The Key to You

Rebecca Hejma

The Key to You
Rebecca Hejma

Copyright © 2026 by Rebecca Hejma

This book contains general information and is not intended to provide medical, legal, financial, or therapeutic advice. Readers should seek the guidance of qualified professionals for any questions or concerns related to the topics discussed.

Every effort has been made to ensure the accuracy of the information contained in this book. The author and publisher assume no responsibility for errors or omissions, or for any consequences arising from the use of the information provided.

ISBN: Paperback 979-8-9944614-0-2

You're welcome to visit my website at **Thekeytoyou.com**

Table of Contents

Chapter 1:

Slowing Down to Reconnect

Somewhere between the rush to keep up and the longing to slow down, we forget what it means to truly live. Reclaiming the inner resources that help us reconnect in a rapidly moving world is not just self-care—it's survival. It's essential for discovering our life's most significant purpose. It's about rediscovering the key to accessing our true selves and beginning the journey toward healing.

I didn't know I was lost until I tried to slow down.

In the blur of deadlines, notifications, and expectations, I thought I was living. I was achieving. I was productive. But beneath the surface, something essential was slipping away—my connection to myself, my purpose, and the quiet truths that once guided me.

It wasn't a dramatic breakdown that woke me up. It was a quiet, aching question that whispered through the noise: *When did I stop listening to my soul?*

1

This book is not about escaping the world. It's about returning to yourself within it. It's about remembering the tools we were all born with—intuition, stillness, presence, and compassion—and learning how to use them again in a world that often rewards distraction over depth.

If you've ever felt like you're moving through life but not truly in it, this is your invitation to pause. To reclaim. To reconnect. Because your purpose isn't out there in the chaos—it's buried within, waiting patiently for you to come home.

The Silence Beneath Everything

There is a silence that lives beneath everything—a deep, sacred stillness that never leaves you, even when you've forgotten how to enter it.

It's there when you wake up with a weight on your chest you can't name.

It's there when your mind races, but your spirit aches for something softer.

It's there in the quiet moments when time slows, and something ancient within you stirs.

This silence is not empty. It is full of memory, meaning, and is the map back to yourself. But our world doesn't honor this silence. It fears it. Distracts from it. Trains us to run from it.

We're handed schedules and apps and metrics instead of moonlight, breath, and presence. The noise has become our normal, and in it, we learned to betray our deepest knowing—and so we drifted.

But even in our forgetting, the tools never left us. The sacred ways of being still live inside you:

- The intuition you were born with
- The breath that connects body to soul
- The ritual of returning again and again to the present moment
- The ability to feel deeply—not as weakness but as power

My Story of Forgetting and Remembering

I know where you're coming from. I've been there. It wasn't until I was in my forties that I finally had the awakening experience of total transformation. Looking back on the previous years of my life, I realized how incomplete and unhappy I had been. I had experienced disconnection—trying to please everyone else, working jobs I despised, tolerating abusive situations, feeling powerless, distrustful, and completely overwhelmed by life.

Why? I asked myself.

Then I began a completely new journey to understand why I had allowed myself to live that way for so many years. I had been giving away my key to everything and everyone except myself and denying myself my own power to be the master of my own kingdom.

As a result of my inner transformation, or as I like to say, finally finding my key, I became a certified life coach because I wanted to be able to help others heal and understand the importance of *The Key to You*. After further training in other modalities, I later opened my spiritual practice.

What followed was a deeper lesson about the illusions I had been climbing toward. The world taught me that life was a ladder, so I kept climbing. Each rung was marked by something measurable: achievement, approval, advancement. I believed that if I just kept going, I would finally reach the place where peace lived. I mistook movement for meaning. I thought the faster I climbed, the closer I'd get to fulfillment.

But the higher I went, the thinner the air became. Not just the air around me but within me. My breath grew shallow. My days blurred. I forgot the sound of my own voice. And then one day, halfway up that invisible ladder, I paused for just a moment and felt an emptiness so deep it startled me.

It wasn't failure. It was something quieter. It was an ancient part of me whispering: *You're going the wrong way.*

That's when I began to descend—slowly, intentionally—not into darkness but into depth. I stepped off the ladder and into the forest. Into the silence. Into the self I had long abandoned in pursuit of something I never really needed.

Invitation to the Reader

This book is written for the one who has climbed long enough to know the summit is a mirage. For the one who aches not for more but for meaning. For the one who is ready to stop chasing and start remembering. Because the truth is, you were never meant to escape this world—you were meant to return to it with sacred awareness, to move differently.

This book is an invitation, not to become someone new but to return to someone ancient—the You who remembers. The You who knows how to live in rhythm with the earth, who walks with purpose not measured in productivity but in presence. Together, we'll remember the tools. We'll unlock the gates. We'll begin the journey home.

As you turn these pages, you'll begin a sacred journey back to yourself. You'll learn how to slow down, listen deeply, and reconnect with the inner tools you may have forgotten: your intuition, your breath, your presence, and your power.

This book will guide you gently but powerfully through the fog of distraction and into clarity, healing, and truth. As you continue reading, you'll discover how to release what no longer serves you, how to live in alignment with your soul, and unlock the radiant purpose that has always lived within you.

By the end, you won't just feel different, you'll be different—living with greater peace, presence, and purpose—grounded, whole, and finally home in yourself.

How to Use This Book

After reclaiming these inner resources that help us reconnect in a rapidly moving world, the next step is to integrate what we've remembered into daily life. With these tools, healing is set into motion, and we become our own sanctuary. Once we've found our key and unlocked ourselves, we no longer seek home—we remember we are the home.

In our fast-paced lives, we can easily become disconnected from our roots and our connection with the Universe. In some cases, we can become totally lost. This book offers tools and reflections to help you reconnect to your life's greater purpose.

Through these pages, you'll unlock your inner self and begin to heal. Together, we'll explore your journey of returning to your authentic self. It's possible to live a life you love, one in which you feel not only happier but healthier within your truth.

Take a deep, hard look at where you are in your life right now. Do you feel lost, depressed, confused, or misaligned? Do you want to let go of all the hopelessness, sadness, feelings of powerlessness, frustration, overwhelm, disconnection, and loneliness? Are you ready to unlock your inner self, clear blocks, heal the past, make real change, feel more empowered, find resolution, and begin living the life you *really* want? By opening your heart and connecting with your inner self, you will find grounding, peace, safety, well-being, and a renewed and fulfilling sense of direction on your journey in life.

Each chapter provides guidance drawn from lived transformation—to inspire, inform, and support you as you learn to live the life you truly love instead of merely settling.

When you release the heaviness of despair and disconnection, your heart opens, and your authentic self rises to the surface. There you will find grounding, peace, safety, well-being, and a new, fulfilled direction through your life.

In this book, you'll explore powerful tools to help you discover the key within you, one that opens the door to healing, clarity, and the life your soul has always desired. These practices are here to guide you back to yourself, to help bring resolution where there's been resistance, and to live with deeper purpose and peace. Keep going. Everything you've been searching for is already within you, and as you move forward, you'll begin to manifest the life that's been waiting for you to remember it.

The journey begins here—with the turning of this page and the gentle unlocking of you.

This is *the key to you.*

Chapter 2:

Awakening from Burnout – Reclaiming the Key to You

It wasn't until I was in my forties that I finally had an awakening—a moment of total transformation. It came after looking back on the previous years of my life, when I never felt complete and happy. I experienced disconnection, constantly trying to please everyone else, working jobs I despised, feeling powerless, putting up with abusive situations, and distrust, and feeling completely overwhelmed by life. One day, I finally stopped and asked myself, *Why?* I was lost for so many years because I never slowed down—I kept giving my key away to others instead of holding it for myself. I thought I was living, but I was slowly disappearing inside the life I refused to change. I was depressed and overwhelmed, and felt a complete disconnection from myself.

This eventually took a major toll on my health and well-being, as I ended up constantly in and out of emergency rooms.

They ran so many tests on me, but found nothing medically wrong. I thought they must be missing something. I decided to leave the big city where I was living and go back home to the Midwest, where I'm originally from. Once I was there, I went to see a specialist at a renowned medical clinic for more testing. Weeks later, I went in for my results and was once again told nothing was wrong. All the tests came back fine. In that moment, I realized the answers I was searching for weren't in a test result—they were within me. It was time to start healing from the inside out.

I had no idea what to do next—I felt in panic mode as I had no answers and no help from any medical doctors. There was no solution to what I was experiencing on a daily basis. I was desperate to find a solution, yet didn't know where to turn next. I was a wreck and found myself wondering, *Am I dying?*

Every day, episodes of these panic attacks and major anxiety caused me to not want to leave the house or even go outside or spend quality time with my family, as I was back home. My heart was racing, my mind was overwhelmed, and I was completely stressed out. All I wanted to do was stay in my bedroom.

Looking back now, I can clearly see that what I was going through was burnout. At the time, I didn't have the language for it—I just knew I was exhausted, anxious, and losing myself. Once I began to understand what burnout really is, I could finally start to heal.

To help others recognize these patterns, I created the acronym BURNOUT to describe the stages and symptoms I experience.

B – Becoming detached: Experiencing emotional distance from work, colleagues, or even loved ones.

U – Unproductive: Feeling a decline in work performance and finding it difficult to complete tasks.

R – Reacting negatively: Exhibiting irritability, cynicism, and a negative outlook.

N – Neglecting self-care: Ignoring personal needs, such as sleep, exercise, or social interactions.

O – Overwhelmed: Feeling constantly stressed, pressured, and unable to cope with demands.

U – Unhappy: Experiencing a general sense of unhappiness, dissatisfaction, and a loss of enjoyment.

T – Tired: Feeling physically, mentally, and emotionally exhausted, with persistent fatigue.

To better understand how burnout shows up in our lives, I began exploring how it affects us on every level—emotionally, behaviorally, mentally, and physically. That's where the ABCs model comes in.

The acronym ABCs, adapted from psychology and stress research, is often used to describe the four ways burnout can show up: **A**ffect (emotions), **B**ehavior (actions), **C**ognition (thoughts), and **S**omatic sensations (physical responses). This framework helps organize and understand the different ways burnout can manifest by categorizing experiences into emotional, behavioral, cognitive, and physical responses.

Here's a breakdown:

Affect: This refers to feelings and moods, like feeling angry, anxious, or depressed.

Behavior: This includes how a person acts in response to burnout, such as withdrawing from social interactions or experiencing increased irritability.

Cognition: This relates to thoughts and thought patterns, like feeling pessimistic or having difficulty concentrating.

Somatic: This encompasses physical sensations and bodily reactions, such as fatigue, headaches, or digestive issues. By examining these four areas, individuals can gain a more comprehensive understanding of their burnout experience and identify potential triggers or coping strategies.

When you begin to realize you have any of these issues, it's time to take action NOW. You must start implementing the techniques I discuss and begin healing yourself. You must be your own hero and find your key to unlock yourself. Without taking action, without making a plan, and without applying the techniques revealed in these pages, the cycle of disconnection only deepens. The weight you feel now will grow heavier, the sense of being lost will expand, and the same struggles in relationships, career, health, and inner peace will continue to repeat themselves. Ignoring your soul's call doesn't make it go away; it only makes the ache louder. But you don't have to keep living this way. By choosing to engage with these tools, you choose healing, clarity, and the possibility of becoming who you were always meant to be.

Bev was experiencing a sense of overwhelm. All she did was put her husband on a pedestal, doing everything for him and never taking time out for herself. She was literally on the brink of a breakdown. She wanted to be the perfect wife, but allowed herself to give her key away. She came to me for help as she did not understand how to break free and why she was like this. I asked her questions to try to get to the root of her problem during a hypnosis session to help her break these chains. It turned out this was a learned behavior, as this is what her grandmother did for her grandfather, although he ended up having an affair and later divorced her grandmother. She has been allowing this behavior as she felt the same thing would end up happening to her and her marriage. After our session, she said, "I almost missed the boat of realization. I know what I need to do now to regain my key and get back to myself."

Can you recognize these blocks showing up in your own life right now? Are there one, three, five, or perhaps even more? Do you catch yourself hoping they'll simply disappear with time? The truth is, they won't. Left unaddressed, they only grow stronger, weaving themselves more deeply into your relationships, your work, your health, and your sense of peace. Change is never easy, and it takes courage to face what's been holding you back. But with the tools I share and the willingness to take that first step, transformation is not only possible, it's also inevitable. You can break free, heal, and finally create the life you truly love and deserve.

You are not alone in this. The blocks you face are not unique to you; countless people today are struggling with the very same feelings of disconnection, overwhelm, and longing for something more. This is part of the shared human experience in our fast-paced world. The good news is, there is a way through. Regaining *the key to you* is a process, and while the journey is deeply personal, you don't have to walk it alone. Within these

11

pages, I've included many different tools and solutions because what resonates for one person may not resonate for another. As you explore, notice which practices speak to you most, and then begin taking action. The moment you start, you've already turned the key and begun your journey back home.

You already hold within you the ability to overcome these blocks and reclaim your key—it has never been lost, only hidden. Even if the path feels overwhelming right now, trust that every step you take will bring you closer to clarity, healing, and freedom. Keep an open mind as you move through these pages because the tools and practices shared here are designed to meet you where you are and guide you forward. Transformation may not happen overnight, but it is absolutely within your reach. With courage, consistency, and the willingness to believe in yourself, you can break through the barriers, unlock your inner self, and begin living the life your soul has been waiting for.

Before we go any further, you might already have a few questions about where to start or what to expect. That's perfectly natural. Change can feel uncertain at first, but curiosity is a sign that you're ready to begin.

How do I even begin to start? You have made the first step by taking the time for yourself to read this book. Now you need to take the time to begin implementing the practices in your everyday routine.

How long does it take to regain my key? Everyone is different. Some will start feeling the rewards quickly, while for others it may take more time and possibly sessions for extra help.

Am I too old? Making positive changes in your life can happen at any age. You just need to want to regain yourself and make the necessary changes by implementing the suggestions I offer.

Have you ever felt like you were living your life for everyone else while slowly losing yourself in the process? You're not alone. So many people give their keys away without even realizing it. The good news is that you can take your key back. With the right tools, you can reconnect with who you are and begin creating the life that truly belongs to you.

Do you catch yourself waiting for the "perfect time" to change, hoping that somehow things will get better on their own? The truth is, there will never be a perfect time, but there is power in starting now. Each small step forward unlocks another door within you, and before you know it, you've begun the transformation you've been craving.

Are you tired of feeling stuck, overwhelmed, and disconnected from your true self? That's exactly why you're here. These feelings are signs calling you back to yourself. Inside these pages, you'll discover the tools to move from stuck to free, from overwhelmed to empowered, and from disconnected to fully alive.

Do you believe deep down that you were meant for more, but you're unsure how to begin? That inner nudge is your soul speaking. It's your reminder that the key has always been within you. By following the steps and practices in this book, you'll finally have a roadmap to unlock your purpose and live with clarity and peace.

No matter where you are right now, remember this: *the key to you* has never been lost. It's been within you all along, waiting for you to turn it. The struggles, setbacks, and blocks you've faced were not meant to break you but to guide you back home to yourself. As you begin to use the tools, insights, and practices shared here, you'll notice that with each step forward, you reclaim more of your power, your purpose, and your peace.

This is your time to rise, to unlock your true self, and to live the life you were always meant to live. The door is right in front of you. Are you ready to turn the key?

I am here to walk beside you on this journey, offering the powerful tools that have transformed my own life and the lives of so many others. Are you ready to begin living the life your soul has always longed for? The practices within these pages are designed to guide you back to your true self, where purpose, peace, and fulfillment naturally flow. Everything you need is already within you; it has been there all along. By embracing these tools and taking the first steps forward, you will begin to manifest the life that has been patiently waiting for you. And when you finally turn the key to unlock yourself fully, you will discover that you already hold everything you've been seeking.

Chapter 3:

Shared Struggles, Shared Hope

Imagine waking up each day with clarity, confidence, and a deep sense of peace, no longer weighed down by overwhelm, anxiety, or self-doubt. Picture yourself moving through life with purpose, setting healthy boundaries, and finally feeling connected to who you truly are. These solutions are not just distant dreams; they are within your reach. By learning how to reclaim your inner key, you can unlock the strength, wisdom, and balance that already exist inside you.

In these pages, I'll share the exact tools and practices that can help you shift from merely surviving to fully thriving, creating a life that feels aligned, fulfilling, and authentically yours.

These are the seven core keys that form the foundation of your transformation:

1. **Taking time for self-care:** nurturing your energy and creating space to listen within

2. **Releasing expectations:** letting go of perfection and external pressure

3. **Grounding yourself and connecting with nature:** restoring calm through the balance of earth and sky

4. **Connecting with your Higher Self:** listening to the wisdom that always guides you

5. **Cleansing your space and working with crystals:** creating an environment that supports healing and clarity

6. **Meditation and activating your Me:** opening pathways to stillness and higher awareness

7. **Energy healing practices:** these include chakra balancing, Reiki, shamanic work, and self-hypnosis: restoring flow, harmony, and wholeness

Each of these keys will open a new doorway of awareness and healing. Together, they create a map that guides you back to balance, clarity, and purpose.

Through both my personal journey and the work I've done with countless clients, I've discovered that there are clear, practical solutions that lead to lasting change.

Now that you've been introduced to the seven keys, it's time to take a closer look at how they work in practice. Each key builds upon the others, creating a foundation for lasting change. You'll soon see that transformation doesn't happen all at once—it happens one mindful step at a time.

The good news is you don't have to guess or struggle alone. These solutions aren't vague ideas or empty promises; they are proven practices that can help you reclaim your power, rediscover your purpose, and restore your inner peace. In the next section, I'll walk you through specific steps and techniques that can be applied immediately to begin your transformation. As I promised in Chapter 1, when you commit to taking action with these tools, the results will be profound—greater understanding, deeper connection, and a life that feels aligned with who you truly are. Let's begin with the first key—taking time for self-care. It forms the foundation for every transformation that follows.

1. Taking Time for Self-Care – *Nurturing Your Energy and Creating Space to Listen Within*

Self-care isn't selfish; it's essential. When you take intentional time for yourself, you replenish your energy, nurture your well-being, and create space to hear your own inner voice. Even small practices like quiet reflection, mindful breathing, or a daily walk can restore balance and remind you of your worth. By choosing self-care, you're not only tending to your body and mind, but you're also strengthening your connection to your soul.

As you begin caring for yourself with greater intention, you may notice the weight of expectations—both your own and those of others—starting to rise to the surface. This is the next step in your transformation: learning to release what no longer serves you.

2. Releasing Expectations – *Letting Go of Perfection and External Pressure*

Expectations, whether from society, family, or even yourself, can feel like invisible chains that keep you from living authentically. When you release them, you free yourself from the weight of trying to measure up to someone else's standards. This doesn't mean giving up on goals or growth, but rather letting go of the pressure to be perfect or to live a life that isn't yours. By releasing expectations, you open the door to acceptance, joy, and the freedom to create a life that feels true to you.

As you release expectations, you create space for something deeper—presence. Letting go of external pressures allows you to reconnect with what's real and enduring. The next step is to return to the natural world, where balance and clarity are always waiting to meet you.

3. Grounding Yourself and Connecting with Nature – *Restoring Calm Through the Balance of Earth and Sky*

Grounding is the practice of anchoring your energy to the present moment and to the earth beneath your feet. When you connect with Mother Earth and Father Sky, you return to a sacred balance between the physical and the spiritual. Spending time in nature, whether it's walking barefoot on the grass, breathing in the forest air, or gazing at the stars, reminds you that you are part of something greater, held in harmony by both earth and sky. Grounding restores your calm, strengthens your energy, and helps you move through life with steadiness and clarity.

As you ground yourself in the natural world, you begin to notice a quiet balance forming within—your energy steadies, and your awareness expands. From this place of calm connection, it becomes easier to tune into a higher level of guidance: the wisdom of your own Higher Self.

4. Connecting with Your Higher Self – *Listening to the Wisdom That Always Guides You*

Your Higher Self is the wise, intuitive part of you that always knows the truth. It's the voice beneath the noise, the guiding light that gently points you toward your soul's purpose. When you quiet the distractions and create space to listen, you strengthen your connection to this inner guidance. Through meditation, stillness, or intentional reflection, you begin to align with your Higher Self, and in that alignment, you find clarity, wisdom, and the courage to live in harmony with your deepest truth.

As you deepen your connection with your Higher Self, you may feel inspired to bring that same sense of clarity and peace into your surroundings. The energy of your environment mirrors your inner state, and by tending to your space, you reinforce the harmony you're cultivating within.

5. Cleansing Your Space and Working with Crystals – *Creating an Environment That Supports Healing and Clarity*

The energy around you is just as important as the energy within you. When your environment is cluttered or filled with stagnant energy, it can weigh heavily on your spirit. Cleansing your space, whether through smudging with sage, using sound such as bells or singing bowls, or simply opening windows to invite in fresh air, helps clear away negativity and restore balance. A cleansed space becomes a sanctuary, supporting your healing, creativity, and connection to your true self.

Crystals are gifts from the earth, each carrying unique vibrations that can support your energy and intentions. From the calming presence of amethyst to the grounding strength of hematite, crystals work as allies in your spiritual journey. They can be used in meditation, placed in your environment, or carried with you to amplify healing and clarity. By working with crystals, you invite their natural wisdom and energy into your life, creating deeper harmony between yourself and the world around you.

As you cleanse your space and attune to the supportive energy of crystals, you begin to notice a greater sense of harmony within and around you. This alignment prepares you for the next step—turning inward through meditation to connect with the vast field of light and awareness that resides at your core.

6. Meditation and Activating Your MerKaBa – *Opening Pathways to Stillness and Higher Awareness*

Meditation

Meditation is the sacred practice of turning inward, quieting the mind, and reconnecting with the stillness that lives at your core. Through meditation, you create space to release stress, listen to your intuition, and realign with your soul's wisdom. Whether it's through breathwork, visualization, or simply sitting in silence, meditation becomes a powerful tool to bring balance, clarity, and peace into your daily life. It is the doorway to presence—and the beginning of hearing your soul's quiet truths.

Activating Your MerKaBa

The MerKaBa is an ancient, divine light vehicle that surrounds your body and connects you to higher realms of consciousness. Activating your MerKaBa allows you to align your energy field with universal love, protection, and spiritual expansion. It is said to bridge the physical and spiritual, helping you access higher awareness, healing, and transformation. Through specific meditations and practices, you awaken this sacred energy field, strengthening your connection to both the earth and the cosmos and empowering you to step fully into your soul's purpose.

As you awaken the light within through meditation and MerKaBa activation, your energy field begins to expand and flow with greater ease. From this heightened state of awareness, you become more attuned to the subtle energies around and within you. The next step is learning to nurture that flow through focused energy-healing practices that restore balance, harmony, and wholeness.

7. Energy Healing Practices – *Restoring Flow, Harmony, and Wholeness*

Chakra Balancing

Your chakras are the body's energy centers, each one linked to a different aspect of your physical, emotional, and spiritual well-being. When these energy points become blocked or unbalanced, it can create feelings of disconnection, fatigue, or disharmony in your life. Chakra balancing works to clear, align, and activate these centers, allowing energy to flow freely once again. When your chakras are in harmony, you feel grounded, centered, and empowered to live with clarity and purpose.

Reiki

Reiki is a gentle yet powerful energy healing practice that channels universal life force energy to promote balance, relaxation, and restoration. By working with this healing energy, Reiki helps dissolve blockages, ease emotional and physical stress, and awaken the body's natural ability to heal itself. It is not about force but about flow, inviting love, light, and harmony back into your mind, body, and spirit. With Reiki, you reconnect to your natural state of peace and wholeness.

Shamanic Healing

Shamanic healing is an ancient practice that helps you reconnect with your soul, clear away energetic blockages, and restore balance on every level of your being. In a session, the shamanic practitioner works with spirit guides, sacred tools, and intuitive wisdom to uncover the root causes of imbalance, whether emotional, physical, or spiritual. These sessions go beyond surface-level healing and reach into the deeper layers of your energy field, bringing clarity, release, and renewal.

Through practices such as soul retrieval, energy clearing, and journeying, shamanic healing opens the doorway to profound transformation. Clients often experience a sense of lightness, emotional release, and a deeper connection to themselves and the universe. By restoring harmony within, shamanic sessions empower you to let go of what no longer serves you and embrace your true essence. It is a sacred path of returning to wholeness, guiding you back to the wisdom, strength, and peace that have always lived inside you.

Hypnosis/Self-Hypnosis

Hypnosis is a gentle, natural state of focused awareness that allows you to quiet the conscious mind and access the deeper layers of your subconscious. In this state, you become more open to positive suggestions and healing, making it easier to release old habits, patterns, and beliefs that may be holding you back. Hypnosis is not about losing control—it's about gaining access to the inner wisdom that already resides within you.

By working directly with the subconscious mind, hypnosis can help you reduce stress, improve confidence, release fears, and create lasting change in your life. Many people describe it as deeply relaxing and empowering, a process where they feel safe, present, and in control while unlocking their ability to transform from within. Hypnosis provides a powerful key to rewriting old stories and embracing new possibilities, guiding you toward the life you truly want to live.

Everything you've just read comes back to the heart of this book: you already hold the key within you. The tools in this chapter, whether it's meditation, grounding, cleansing your space, or connecting with your Higher Self, are not just practices; they are doorways back to your power, your purpose, and your peace. Each one is designed to help you release what no longer serves you and step into the life you've been longing for. When you begin to use these tools consistently, even in small ways, the shifts can be profound.

I know this because I've lived it myself. There was a time when I felt disconnected, overwhelmed, and unsure of my path. By applying these practices, I began to heal, align with my purpose, and experience a deeper sense of fulfillment than I ever thought possible. I've also witnessed countless clients step into their power, release old blocks, and transform their lives through these very same tools. The same is possible for you. Keep reading with an open heart; you're not just learning techniques, you're stepping into a journey of remembering who you truly are. The best is yet to come, and your transformation is already unfolding.

Your journey begins with the first key: taking time for self-care. When you open it, every other key will begin to unlock naturally.

Before you can move fully into growth, you must first return to yourself. The next chapter invites you to slow down, release the expectations that weigh you down, and rediscover the calm strength that comes from caring for your own well-being. This is where healing takes root—one breath, one choice, one act of self-kindness at a time.

Chapter 4:

Self-Care and Releasing Expectations

Key 1. Taking time for self-care: nurturing your energy and creating space to listen within

Key 2. Releasing expectations: letting go of perfection and external pressure

When Megan booked an energy healing session, her energy felt heavy and burdened by exhaustion and emotion. She described feeling completely drained, as if life had stripped her of all vitality, "like a vampire sucked out all my blood," she said. The weight of family, work, and constant expectations had left her feeling trapped and powerless. As I tuned into her energy, I sensed deep blockages and layers of exhaustion that had built up over time. What stood out most was the absence of self-care; Megan had been giving endlessly to everyone around her, leaving nothing for herself.

During our session, I worked to gently clear those blockages and guide her back toward balance. We released stagnant energy and invited light and renewal into the spaces where heaviness once lived. As the session unfolded, I could feel her energy begin to shift. Her breathing deepened, her body relaxed, and her spirit started to feel lighter. By the end, Megan described feeling free, uplifted, and as though a tremendous weight had been lifted off her shoulders. She left not only with a renewed sense of strength but also with tools to prioritize self-care and release unrealistic expectations. Her transformation was a beautiful reminder that when we return to our own inner power, healing is always possible.

You may recognize parts of yourself in Megan's story, but allowing yourself to get to this point is quite unhealthy on many levels. If you're not taking time for self-care, you must start now, as it's essential. It can be as simple as a daily walk, surrounding yourself with nature, sitting quietly, and reflecting. Ask yourself, "When was the last time I did this? How often do I make space for it? Are expectations from others hindering you to the point that you feel as if you have chains around you, weighing you down? Is the pressure of life overwhelming you?

Megan's story is powerful because it reflects what so many of us quietly endure: giving too much of ourselves, ignoring our own needs, and eventually reaching a breaking point. Her experience shows that when we neglect self-care and carry the heavy weight of constant expectations, our energy, health, and sense of peace begin to crumble. The good news is, you don't have to wait until you feel completely drained to make a change. Simple, intentional practices—like taking a daily walk, reconnecting with nature, or setting aside quiet time for reflection—can begin restoring your balance and vitality right now. Ask yourself, "Am I giving to everyone but myself?" If expectations from others feel like chains holding you down, it's a sign to shift your focus inward. By releasing those pressures and committing to small, consistent acts of self-care, you begin unlocking the very key that brings you back to your true self.

Try This Now

Take out a journal and write down three ways you can nurture yourself this week, big or small. It might be something as simple as enjoying a quiet cup of tea, taking a walk without your phone, or saying "No" to an obligation that drains you. Then circle the one that feels most doable today and commit to it. Notice how even one small act of self-care begins to shift your energy and lighten the weight you've been carrying.

Invitation Exercise: Releasing Expectations

Take a quiet moment to sit with yourself, free from distractions. Close your eyes, breathe deeply, and bring to mind one expectation you feel weighing heavily on you right now. It could be from work, family, friends, or even yourself. Notice how this expectation feels in your body. Does it feel tight in your chest, heavy on your shoulders, or like a knot in your stomach?

Now, place your hand over your heart and ask yourself, "Is this expectation truly mine, or is it something I've been carrying for someone else?" If it doesn't belong to you, imagine gently setting it down. Visualize placing it into a river, allowing the current to carry it away, or picture unlocking chains and stepping free.

Write in your journal:

1. Whose expectations have I been carrying that no longer serve me?
2. What is one expectation I can lovingly release today?
3. How can I replace it with compassion and freedom for myself?

When you release just one expectation, you create space for peace, authenticity, and alignment to flow in.

It's one thing to understand the importance of self-care, but it's another to truly embody it in your daily life. To help you reconnect with yourself, let's begin with a simple exercise that invites you to pause, listen, and honor your own needs.

Invitation Exercise: Returning to Self-Care

Find a comfortable place where you won't be interrupted. Close your eyes and take three slow, deep breaths. With each inhale, imagine breathing in light and nourishment. With each exhale, release the stress and tension you've been holding. Now, gently ask yourself, "What is one small act of care my body, mind, or spirit is asking for today?" Trust the first thought or image that comes to you; it might be rest, movement, stillness, or creativity. Write it down. Then, commit to giving yourself this act of care within the next 24 hours.

Journal Prompts

1. When was the last time I truly honored my own needs?
2. How do I feel when I take even ten minutes just for me?

Releasing expectations is not just a mental idea—it's an energetic shift that creates freedom and peace. To begin practicing this, I invite you to an exercise that will help you identify what no longer belongs to you and let it go with love.

Invitation Exercise: Releasing Expectations

Sit quietly with your journal and a pen. Take a few breaths and bring to mind an expectation that feels especially heavy, whether from yourself, a loved one, or society. Write it down at the top of the page.

Next, ask yourself, "Is this expectation truly mine, or have I taken it on for someone else?" Beneath the expectation, write what it has cost you: peace, energy, freedom, and joy. Then, on a new line, write: "I now release this expectation with love. I choose freedom instead."

Tear out the page, fold it, and either burn it safely, bury it, or place it under a stone outdoors as a symbolic act of letting it go.

Journal Prompts

1. Whose voice is behind this expectation?
2. What would my life feel like without it?

The Sacred Pause

Step 1: Set a timer for five minutes. Put away your phone and remove distractions.

Step 2: Sit comfortably, place one hand on your heart and the other on your belly.

Step 3: Breathe deeply and ask yourself, "What do I need in this moment?" Don't judge the answer. Whether it's rest, water, movement, or quiet, simply honor it.

Step 4: After the five minutes, write down your answer and take one small action to fulfill that need before the day ends.

This practice helps you build trust with yourself by listening and responding to your body's whispers before they become screams.

The Joy List Ritual

Step 1: Take a blank page and write at the top: "Things that make me feel alive and nourished."

Step 2: List ten simple joys (like taking a bath, reading in silence, walking barefoot in grass, or cooking a favorite meal).

Step 3: Circle three things and commit to doing at least one this week.

Over time, your Joy List becomes your personal self-care map, something you can turn to whenever you feel disconnected or drained.

Releasing Expectations Exercises

The Expectation Release Journal

Step 1: On one side of a page, write down expectations you feel from others (family, work, society, etc.).

Step 2: On the other side, write what you truly want instead.

Step 3: Draw a line through the expectations that don't align with your heart and say aloud, "I release this. It no longer defines me."

This helps you see clearly which pressures are external and gives you permission to reclaim your own voice.

The "Should-Free Day" Challenge

Step 1: Choose one day this week to live without the word "should."

Step 2: Anytime you catch yourself thinking "I should…," pause and ask, "Do I actually want this or is it someone else's expectation?"

Step 3: Replace the thought with "I choose to…" or "I release this for now."

This exercise rewires your language and mindset, helping you notice how often expectations drive your choices and giving you space to choose differently.

As you try living a "should-free" day, you may begin to notice just how often those quiet demands shape your thoughts and choices. For some, these realizations appear subtly; for others, they come as a wake-up call. Samantha's story shows what can happen when those expectations go unchecked—and how transformation begins the moment we decide to let them go.

Samantha was the type of person who did everything for everyone. At work, she stayed late to finish projects that weren't even hers. At home, she cared for her children, her husband, and even her aging parents, rarely stopping to breathe for herself. From the outside, people admired her. "She's so strong, she can handle anything." But inside, Samantha was unraveling. She was exhausted, resentful, and quietly whispering to herself at night, "When is it my turn?"

It wasn't until her body finally forced her to stop when she broke down in tears at the kitchen sink one evening that she realized something had to change. Samantha booked a healing session, and during our work together, it became clear that she had given away her energy to meet everyone else's expectations and left nothing for her own care. Through simple daily self-care practices, like carving out ten quiet minutes for herself in the morning, and through the powerful act of releasing the "shoulds" she had been carrying from others, Samantha began to feel lighter. She discovered that when she cared for herself first, she could show up with more love, presence, and balance for those she cared about.

Her story is a reminder for all of us: you cannot pour from an empty cup. Self-care is not selfish, and releasing expectations is not failure. It is freedom. By reclaiming your energy and your choices, you begin to unlock the life you were meant to live, full of peace, purpose, and vitality.

Samantha's story shows what happens when we forget to include ourselves in the circle of our own care. Now it's your turn to begin that same shift, one small, intentional choice at a time. The following practice offers a simple way to remember what self-care truly means and how to bring it into your daily life.

SELF-CARE

S – Slow Down → Give yourself permission to pause and breathe.

E – Embrace Rest → Honor your body's need for sleep and rejuvenation.

L – Listen Within → Tune into your intuition and inner guidance.

F – Fuel Your Body → Nourish yourself with healthy food, movement, and water.

C – Create Boundaries → Protect your energy by saying "No" when needed.

A – Allow Joy → Make space for play, laughter, and activities that bring you lightness.

R – Release Expectations → Let go of shoulds and embrace what feels true to you.

E – Engage Spiritually → Connect with practices that ground you—meditation, nature, prayer, or stillness.

Each part of SELF-CARE is more than an idea. It's a daily invitation to return to yourself. In the following pages, you'll take a closer look at what each letter represents and how these simple practices can help you create balance, presence, and renewal in your everyday life.

S – Slow Down

Life moves fast, but your soul moves at the pace of presence. Slowing down is where healing begins.

Practice: Take three deep breaths before every new task today. Let each exhale remind you that you don't have to rush.

E – Embrace Rest

Rest is not laziness—it's renewal. When you honor your body with sleep and stillness, your energy expands.
Practice: Tonight, give yourself permission to go to bed thirty minutes earlier than usual. No screens, just quiet, nourishing rest.

L – Listen Within

Your inner wisdom is always speaking, but you must create silence to hear it.

Practice: Sit quietly for five minutes, hand on your heart, and ask, "What do I most need today?" Write down the first answer that comes.

F – Fuel Your Body

What you eat and drink and how you move shapes how you feel. Choose nourishment, not punishment.

Practice: Add one extra glass of water or one nutrient-rich food to your meals today. Celebrate it as a loving act, not an obligation.

C – Create Boundaries

Boundaries are sacred—they protect your energy and make room for peace.

Practice: Say "No" once this week when you would normally say "Yes" out of guilt. Notice how empowering it feels.

A – Allow Joy

Joy is medicine. Play, laughter, and lightness raise your vibration and heal your spirit.

Practice: Do one small thing today that sparks joy—dance to a song, laugh with a friend, or savor a favorite treat.

R – Release Expectations

Expectations from others are chains that weigh you down. Freedom comes when you let go.

Practice: Write down one expectation (from yourself or others) that no longer serves you. Rip it up or burn it as an act of release.

E – Engage Spiritually

True self-care is remembering you are connected—to Spirit, to nature, to something greater than yourself.

Practice: Spend ten minutes outdoors noticing the earth and sky. Whisper a simple gratitude: "I am connected, I am supported, and I am grateful."

When you practice SELF-CARE, you return to yourself piece by piece. These small steps build into a powerful transformation—reminding you that you are worthy, whole, and already have the key within.

As you deepen your practice of SELF-CARE, you naturally begin to notice what no longer fits, such as old habits, expectations, and pressures that keep you from peace. The next step in your journey is learning how to release these burdens with compassion and courage. The following framework, RELEASE, will guide you through that process.

RELEASE – A Path to Freedom from Expectations

R – Recognize the Weight → Notice where expectations are draining your energy.

E – Examine the Source → Ask, "Is this mine, or did it come from others (family, society, work)?"

L – Let Go of "shoulds" → Replace "I should" with "I choose" or "I release."

E – Embrace Self-Compassion → Be gentle with yourself: progress, not perfection, matters.

A – Align with Truth → Reconnect with what feels authentic to your soul.

S – Surrender Control → Trust the Universe to hold what you cannot.

E – Empower Your Freedom → Celebrate the lightness that comes from living on your terms.

Now that you've seen the steps of the RELEASE framework, take a moment to pause and reflect. Each part is designed to help you let go of what no longer serves you so you can live with greater lightness and authenticity. Let's begin by recognizing the weight you've been carrying because awareness is the first step toward freedom.

R – Recognize the Weight

You cannot release what you don't first acknowledge. Awareness is the beginning of freedom.

Practice: Write down three expectations (your own or others) that feel heavy. Circle the one that drains you the most.

E – Examine the Source
Many expectations aren't even ours; they're inherited from family, culture, or society.

Practice: Next to each expectation, ask, "Whose voice is this really?" Write the answer honestly, even if it surprises you.

L – Let Go of "Shoulds"
Replace "I should" with "I choose" or "I release."

E – Embrace Self-Compassion
Be gentle with yourself; progress, not perfection, matters.

A – Align with Truth
Reconnect with what feels authentic to your soul.

S – Surrender Control
Trust the Universe to hold what you cannot.

E – Empower Your Freedom
Celebrate the lightness that comes from living on your terms.

As you move through each step of RELEASE, remember that this process isn't theoretical—it's deeply human. Every "should" you let go of, and every truth you reclaim brings you closer to peace. To see how this unfolds in real life, let's look at a story that beautifully illustrates the power of releasing expectations and reclaiming self-care.

When Megan came to me for an energy healing session, she felt completely drained, like a vampire had taken all her strength. What we uncovered was not just exhaustion, but a complete lack of self-care and the crushing weight of others' expectations. Her story is exactly why practices like SELF-CARE and RELEASE matter. If Megan had paused to listen to herself, or if she had given herself permission to release the "shoulds" that weren't hers to carry, her energy wouldn't have reached the breaking point it did. By gradually weaving these practices into her life, Megan learned that healing was possible because every time she chose herself, she unlocked a piece of her freedom.

Samantha's story also shows us the cost of ignoring these steps. She poured into everyone else until her body forced her to stop. It was only when she began creating boundaries and aligning with her truth that her healing began. For her, the RELEASE framework was a lifeline, recognizing the weight she carried, examining where it came from, and finally surrendering the need to meet everyone's expectations. These small but intentional acts gave her permission to rest, to breathe, and to reclaim her energy.

Bev, too, had allowed generational patterns of over-giving to define her. She believed being the "perfect wife" meant carrying everything, but it left her broken and resentful. Her turning point came when she realized she had been giving away her key. The solution wasn't complicated; it was about remembering the tools she already had. For her, self-care meant allowing joy again, and releasing expectations meant empowering her freedom. With these steps, she began writing a new story, not one of sacrifice, but one of balance, love, and peace.

These stories are not unique to Megan, Samantha, or Bev. They are reflections of what so many of us silently endure. But the truth is, you don't have to wait for breakdowns or exhaustion to reclaim your key. The how-to steps of SELF-CARE and RELEASE give you a map. They are not lofty ideas—they are practical, daily choices that create space for healing. And just like Megan, Samantha, and Bev, when you choose to walk this path, your story, too, will transform.

The stories you've just read, and the steps I've given you through SELF-CARE and RELEASE, are not just nice concepts. They are living, breathing examples of how reclaiming your key is possible in real life. You already hold the key to unlocking your inner self, which is proven when you put these practices into action. Each step is a doorway that brings you closer to the life you desire: one filled with balance, freedom, and peace.

You can apply this right now by looking at your own life. Where are you giving away your key? Is it in saying "Yes" when you want to say "No"? Is it in carrying expectations that don't belong to you? Is it in neglecting your body, your spirit, or your rest? By practicing even one part of SELF-CARE or RELEASE, you begin the process of reclaiming that key. This isn't about perfection; it's about taking consistent, small actions that bring you back to your power. When you do, you'll notice the shift: more energy, more clarity, more peace. And this is just the beginning. Keep going, and you will manifest the promises of this book because *the key to you* has always been within.

As you continue with these steps, you'll begin to see the promises of this journey unfolding. The overwhelm will loosen its grip, replaced by clarity and calm. The weight of expectations will lift, allowing you to feel lighter, freer, and more connected to your true self. By practicing self-care and learning to release what no longer serves you, you're not only healing the present, you're creating a foundation for lasting peace, purpose, and empowerment. Every choice to honor yourself is a step toward unlocking the life that's been waiting for you. Keep moving forward with these tools, and you'll discover that the fulfillment you've been searching for has been within you all along—your key, your power, and your freedom.

You've learned to nurture yourself through self-care and to free yourself by releasing the expectations that weigh you down. The next step is to anchor these inner shifts in something steady and real. In the chapters ahead, you'll discover how grounding in nature and connecting with your Higher Self deepen everything you've begun here. These practices root your healing in presence, strengthen your clarity, and remind you that balance isn't found in doing more—it's found in remembering who you truly are.

Chapter 5:

Grounding Yourself, Embracing Nature, & Connecting with Your Higher Self

---

Key 3. Grounding yourself and connecting with nature: restoring calm through the balance of earth and sky

Key 4. Connecting with your Higher Self: listening to the wisdom that always guides you

---

Many years ago, when I was living in the hustle and bustle of city life, I didn't realize the importance of grounding and connecting with nature. Yes, there were times I'd drive out to a secluded area just to see some different scenery or take a walk, but back then, I didn't understand what grounding truly meant. I thought it was simply "getting a break." I didn't know it was about walking barefoot on the earth, breathing deeply in the fresh air, or even hugging a tree, making a conscious connection with Mother Earth and Father Sky. Had I known the power of grounding at that time, I might have felt calmer, less anxious, more energized and clearer. Instead, the constant rush and endless motion eventually caught up to me, leading to severe panic attacks.

It wasn't until physical ailments began to surface and after endless medical tests with no real answers that I turned inward, searching for solutions. That's when I discovered the practices I now share with you. Back then, I didn't even know what a Higher Self was. Sure, I believed in God and prayed, but the noise of my distracted life drowned out the deeper connection waiting for me. Through spiritual study, healing practices, and eventually classes, I uncovered what I had been missing all those years. My ego had been running the show, but once I began removing distractions, I opened the doorway to my Higher Self. It took time and practice, but that connection became a source of truth and clarity that has never misled me. It was and continues to be life-changing. I encourage you to devote time to building your own sacred relationship with your Higher Self. It will awaken a deeper wisdom within you, fill you with peace, and help you feel more enlightened than you ever imagined possible.

My story is meant to show you that sometimes we don't realize what we're missing until life forces us to stop and pay attention. I had to learn the hard way through anxiety, panic attacks, and physical ailments, but you don't have to wait for things to spiral that far. By practicing grounding and intentionally connecting with your Higher Self, you give yourself the gift of stability, clarity, and inner peace before life demands it. These practices are simple yet profound, and they remind you that the answers you seek are not "out there"; they're already within you, waiting to be unlocked. As you begin to weave grounding and

Higher Self connection into your daily life, you'll notice shifts in your energy, your resilience, and your sense of purpose. This is how you reclaim your key and step into the calm, balanced, and empowered life you were always meant to live.

Invitation Exercise: Ground & Connect with Your Higher Self

Find Your Space – Step outside if possible, somewhere quiet in nature. If not, sit comfortably indoors with your feet flat on the ground.

Ground Yourself – Close your eyes, take three deep breaths, and imagine roots growing from the soles of your feet deep into the earth. Feel Mother Earth holding you steady, safe, and supported.

Release the Noise – With each exhale, let go of stress, expectations, and distractions. Imagine them flowing down into the earth to be recycled into light.

Connect Upward – Now, imagine a soft golden light above your head, the wisdom of Father Sky, and your Higher Self. Allow this light to gently flow down into you, filling your heart and mind with clarity, peace, and truth.

Ask & Listen – Silently ask your Higher Self, "What do I need most right now?" Stay still for a few moments and notice what arises, whether it's a feeling, a word, or a sense of calm.

Close with Gratitude – Thank yourself for taking this sacred time. Place a hand over your heart and affirm, "I am grounded, guided, and connected to my true self."

Quick Daily Grounding (5 Minutes)

Perfect for mornings, lunch breaks, or before bed.

Pause & Breathe – Take three slow, deep breaths, feeling your body relax.

Ground – Imagine roots growing from your feet deep into the earth.

Release – On each exhale, let go of stress, expectations, or worry.

Connect – Visualize a golden light above your head flowing into your heart.

Affirm – Place your hand over your chest and whisper, "I am grounded, guided, and at peace."

Deeper Grounding & Higher Self Connection (10–15 Minutes)

Ideal for weekends, after a stressful day, or when you want to go deeper.

Create Sacred Space – Light a candle, burn incense, or sit outside in nature.

Ground Fully – Close your eyes and breathe deeply. Imagine roots extending from your body into Mother Earth, anchoring you firmly. Feel her strength rise up through your legs.

Release Expectations – Visualize chains or heavy weights falling away from your shoulders into the earth, dissolving into light.

Connect to Higher Self – Picture a brilliant golden or white light above your crown. Allow it to flow into you, filling your mind and heart with truth and clarity.

Ask for Guidance – Silently ask, "What truth does my Higher Self want me to know right now?" Be still. Notice any words, feelings, or images.

Integrate & Give Thanks – When ready, place your hands over your heart and affirm, "I am connected, I am whole, I am guided." Carry this calm energy with you into your day.

Journal Prompts for Quick Daily Grounding

After completing the 5-minute practice, write:

1. What do I feel in my body right now compared to before I began?
2. What is one expectation, thought, or worry I released in this moment?
3. What is one small way I can show myself care today?

Jot down even a few quick sentences. This creates daily awareness and progress.

Journal Prompts for Deeper Grounding & Higher Self Connection

After completing the 10–15-minute practice, write:

1. What message, symbol, or feeling did my Higher Self share with me today?
2. Where in my life am I holding expectations that no longer serve me?
3. How can I honor myself more fully in the days ahead?
4. What steps will I take to stay grounded when life feels overwhelming?

Have you been convincing yourself that pushing harder, doing more, and racing through the noise of life is the only way to succeed? Be honest, has it really brought you peace, or has it left you anxious, scattered, and disconnected from your true self? The old way of ignoring your body, rushing past your needs, and living only in your head isn't working anymore. It's not making you stronger; it's uprooting you. What if instead, you grounded yourself literally and spiritually by slowing down, breathing deeply, walking barefoot on the earth, and reconnecting to the stability of Mother Earth and Father Sky? This new path will restore your balance, calm your nervous system, and bring you back to a place of strength that no amount of "doing" can ever give.

Look inside yourself for a moment: are you truly living the life you desire, or are you living the one others expect of you? If you're honest, you may realize you've been guided by fear, ego, and endless demands rather than by the quiet wisdom of your Higher Self. But here's the challenge: the old way of ignoring that inner voice, of silencing your soul's whispers, is no longer sustainable, and deep down, you know it. The good news is, there is another way. By releasing expectations and learning to connect with your Higher Self, you'll begin to see truth more clearly, make decisions with confidence, and walk a path aligned with your deepest purpose. This sacred connection is your compass back home.

Samantha came to me during a season of her life when everything felt unsteady. She described herself as constantly "spinning," like she was on a merry-go-round that never stopped. Her days were full of work deadlines, family obligations, and endless distractions, but no matter how much she accomplished, she felt empty and disconnected inside. She admitted she hadn't taken a quiet walk in nature in years, and prayer or meditation seemed like luxuries she didn't have time for. The stress had begun to show up in her body—tight shoulders, sleepless nights, and constant fatigue. During our sessions together, I introduced her to simple grounding practices, walking barefoot in her yard, breathing deeply with intention, and taking a few quiet minutes outdoors each day to reconnect with the earth. At first, it felt almost too simple to her, but soon she began noticing how much calmer and clearer she felt after these moments. From there, we began working on connecting with her Higher Self.

Through guided meditations, Samantha began to hear her own inner wisdom truths, which had been buried under the noise of expectations. She realized she had been making choices based on fear and obligation rather than alignment with her true self. As she learned to ground daily and tune into her Higher Self, she found clarity about her next steps in life, released a job that was draining her, and began pursuing creative passions that lit her up. Samantha later told me, "It feels like I finally came home to myself."

A few years ago, I worked with Daniel, who came to me feeling completely unmoored. He described his life as if he were "floating in a storm with no anchor." His job consumed him, his relationships felt strained, and no matter how much he accomplished, he carried a constant sense of restlessness and emptiness. When he sat down with me, I could feel how ungrounded he was; his energy was scattered, like pieces of himself pulled in a hundred different directions. He admitted that he hadn't spent any real time in nature in years and that quiet moments of self-reflection were almost nonexistent in his daily life. His entire world was built on busyness, but underneath it all, he was searching for something deeper.

During our work together, I guided Daniel through grounding practices, walking barefoot in the grass, breathing deeply with awareness, and reconnecting with the stability of the earth beneath him. At first, he thought it sounded too simple to matter, but within weeks, he noticed a change: his anxiety began to soften, his sleep improved, and he felt calmer in situations that once triggered him. From there, we moved into connecting with his Higher Self. Through meditation and intentional stillness, Daniel began to hear his own inner wisdom more clearly. He described it as "tuning into a frequency that had always been there, but I never slowed down enough to listen." This connection brought him awareness about his purpose, renewed his sense of trust in life, and gave him the confidence to make choices that truly aligned with his soul. Grounding gave him stability; his Higher Self gave him direction. Together, they became the key to unlocking the peace he had been seeking for years.

To experience the calm, clarity, and guidance that Samantha discovered, you must take intentional action every day. Start by grounding yourself—walk barefoot on the earth, breathe deeply with awareness, or simply sit outside and notice the sights, sounds, and sensations of nature. These simple practices reconnect you with Mother Earth and Father Sky, anchoring your energy and releasing tension that builds from constant stress. Next, cultivate a relationship with your Higher Self. This requires stillness, openness, and curiosity: meditate, journal, or sit quietly and ask for guidance. Pay attention to the subtle insights, feelings, or inner nudges that arise, even if they feel small or uncertain at first. Above all, approach this practice with patience and self-compassion, knowing that establishing this connection is a journey, not a one-time event. By consistently grounding yourself and tuning into your Higher Self, you will develop the clarity, inner strength, and wisdom to make aligned choices and create a life that truly resonates with your soul.

1. Begin with Grounding

Spend 5–10 minutes each day outside.

Walk barefoot on the grass, soil, or sand if possible.

Close your eyes, breathe deeply, and imagine your energy flowing down into the earth, anchoring you in stability and strength.

As you exhale, release stress, tension, and any heavy emotions into the ground to be transmuted.

Reflection prompt: How does my body feel after grounding compared to before?

2. Quiet the Noise

Find a quiet space where you won't be disturbed.

Sit comfortably, close your eyes, and take a few slow, steady breaths.

Place your hands on your heart and silently set the intention: "I open myself to hear and connect with my Higher Self."

Reflection prompt: What thoughts, images, or feelings arise as I create this space of stillness?

3. Ask & Listen

Ask your Higher Self a simple question, such as:

1) What do I need most right now?

2) What expectation can I release today?

3) What is my next step toward peace?

Don't force an answer. Allow guidance to come as a feeling, a thought, or even a sense of knowing.

Reflection prompts: What guidance did I receive? How can I apply it today?

4. Act with Intention

Choose one small action each day to honor what you received, whether that's saying "No," resting, journaling, or taking a walk.

Remember: wisdom without action fades away.

Reflection prompt: What action will I take today to honor my Higher Self?

The practices of grounding and connecting with your Higher Self are not just spiritual exercises; they are practical tools to help you reclaim your key and step fully into the life you desire. If you've been feeling scattered, anxious, or disconnected from your purpose, these steps meet those exact needs. By intentionally grounding yourself, you release tension, gain clarity, and stabilize your energy so you can navigate life with confidence. By connecting with your Higher Self, you access the wisdom, guidance, and inner knowing that has always been within you.

Applied consistently, these practices help you align with your true self, make empowered choices, and create a life filled with peace, purpose, and fulfillment. In essence, they are the bridge between where you are now and the life you've been longing for, your key to unlocking your inner self. By choosing to ground yourself and connect with your Higher Self, you are saying "Yes" to clarity, peace, and a deeper sense of purpose. These steps are not abstract ideas but practical actions that, when practiced with consistency, will bring you more calm, balance, and direction in your daily life. The promises of living with greater energy, freedom from overwhelm, and alignment with your true purpose are not far-off dreams; they are the natural results of doing this inner work. As you continue forward, know that every moment you spend grounding and listening to your Higher Self brings you closer to unlocking your key and living the life you've always known was possible.

As you strengthen your connection with the earth and your Higher Self, the next natural step is to align your outer world with your inner growth. The spaces you live, work, and rest in carry energy just as your body and spirit do. When that energy becomes stagnant or cluttered, it can quietly drain your strength and clarity. In the next chapter, we'll explore how to cleanse and elevate your environment—physically and energetically—so it supports the peace, balance, and purpose you've begun to cultivate within.

Chapter 6:

Cleansing Your Space and Crystals

Key 5. Cleansing your space and working with crystals: creating an environment that supports healing and clarity

---

I eventually discovered the importance of cleansing and working with crystals. It wasn't just about clearing the energy in my home, car, or new items I brought into my space; it was also about cleansing myself. I noticed how heavy I felt after being around negative people or environments, and I knew I had to release that energy. Beyond that, I realized the deeper work was cleansing my life of people and objects that no longer served my highest good. Letting go of unhealthy relationships, whether lifelong friends, family members, or toxic influences I had allowed in, was not easy—but it was necessary.

The truth is, the energy around you can weigh you down just as much as the energy within you.

That's when I began using sage, starting at my front door and moving in a clockwise direction through each room, always leaving a window open so the stagnant energy had a way to escape. I also discovered palo santo, which not only clears away negativity but also invites positivity. Over time, I incorporated bells and singing bowls, each bringing its own unique vibration of cleansing.

Around this same period, I was introduced to crystals, and they became an essential part of my spiritual journey. Cleansed and charged crystals hold energy that supports your intentions and harmonizes your spirit. I began carrying them in my pocket, wearing them as jewelry, and using them in meditation. Later, I explored creating crystal grids to align with specific outcomes I wanted to manifest. I was amazed at the benefits: they felt alive, offering wisdom and balance. Just as we must cleanse ourselves, crystals must also be cleansed of prior energies they may carry. I now program each of my crystals with intention, though that practice is optional. For me, combining cleansing rituals with the power of crystals has been truly transformative, opening the door to deeper healing and alignment.

This story shows that cleansing your space, your energy, and even your relationships is not just a ritual; it's a powerful act of self-care and alignment. When you release what no longer serves you, whether it's stagnant energy, toxic connections, or old objects carrying heavy vibrations, you create room for healing, clarity, and peace to flow into your life. Crystals, sage, palo santo, and other tools are not simply spiritual accessories; they are allies that can support your intentions and raise your vibration. By learning to cleanse both your environment and yourself, and by incorporating the supportive energy of crystals, you too can lighten the emotional and energetic weight you've been carrying. This solution helps you reconnect with your true self and live from a place of greater balance, strength, and purpose.

Have you ever walked into a room and instantly felt drained, heavy, or uneasy, even if nothing looked wrong? Or noticed how certain people in your life leave you feeling exhausted, while others lift you up? The truth is, energy is real, and it impacts you far more than you realize. If you've been ignoring the heaviness of your environment or clinging to toxic relationships and clutter that no longer serve you, then it's no wonder you feel stuck, anxious, or dragged down.

The old way, pushing through, pretending it doesn't matter, or numbing yourself, is not working. Those choices only bury you deeper in the very energy that's keeping you from living with peace and clarity. So let me ask you, are you truly willing to keep carrying all that weight, or are you ready to release it and make room for the life you deserve?

It's time to take a new direction. Cleansing your space, your energy, and even your relationships is not a luxury; it's a necessity if you want to feel light, focused, and aligned. Crystals, sage, palo santo, and other powerful tools are here to support you, not just as objects but as partners in raising your vibration and protecting your spirit.

By learning how to clear away what drains you and surrounding yourself with energy that uplifts you, you can reclaim your sense of harmony and step fully into your purpose. This chapter will guide you through practices and perspectives that empower you to let go of what weighs you down so you can finally live with the clarity, balance, and freedom you've been searching for. The question is, are you ready to choose freedom, clarity, and balance over the chaos that has held you back?

Anna came to me feeling completely overwhelmed. She explained that no matter what she did, she felt overloaded by the energy in her own home. She was exhausted and irritable and even found herself avoiding her space because it felt "too heavy." As we talked, I could sense that she had taken on a lot of energy that wasn't hers. Between her demanding job, stressful family dynamics, and the constant busyness of life, her space had become cluttered not only with physical things but with stagnant, negative energy. I suggested we begin with a simple cleansing ritual, teaching her how to use sage to clear her home while also introducing her to the grounding and supportive energy of crystals.

When Anna began incorporating these practices, she noticed a shift almost immediately. After her first cleansing, she described the air in her home as "lighter" and even said she could breathe more deeply. She chose a few crystals that resonated with her: rose quartz for self-love, black tourmaline for protection, and clear quartz to amplify her intentions. Within weeks, she shared how much calmer she felt and that being in her own space felt safe and nurturing again.

She began to see that cleansing and crystals weren't just rituals but tools to release what was weighing her down and to support her in creating a space filled with peace and balance. Anna's story shows that when we consciously clear and protect our energy, we make room for healing, clarity, and the freedom to move forward with a lighter spirit.

To benefit from the practices of cleansing and working with crystals, the first step is awareness. Begin by noticing how your space feels. Do you walk into your home and immediately feel relaxed, or do you sense tension, heaviness, or even irritation? Our environments hold energy, and that energy directly affects our mood, health, and clarity. Once you become aware of how a space feels, you can begin to shift it with intentional cleansing.

Start with a simple cleansing ritual. Gather a cleansing tool such as sage or palo santo. Light it safely and allow the smoke to move gently through your space. Having a feather and an abalone shell greatly helps with this, as you can fan the smoke while the lit sage or palo santo is in the shell. Begin at your front door and work clockwise through each room, paying extra attention to corners, windows, and areas where you spend a lot of time. As you do this, set a clear intention, something like, "I release all negative energy and invite in peace, light, and clarity." Open a window or door so the stagnant energy has somewhere to go. This is not just about smoke and ritual; it's about aligning your intention with your environment and creating a fresh, energetic foundation.

Once your space is cleansed, it's time to introduce crystals. Crystals are natural allies that hold specific vibrations, and when we use them intentionally, they can help support our emotional, spiritual, and even physical well-being. Choose crystals that resonate with your current needs. For example, amethyst for calm and intuition, rose quartz for love and compassion, or black tourmaline for grounding and protection.

The key practice you need to cultivate is consistency. Cleansing your space or carrying a crystal once may feel refreshing, but real transformation comes when these practices become part of your lifestyle. Make it a habit to cleanse your home weekly or after guests and carry or meditate with your crystals daily. This steady practice not only clears away negativity but also builds a protective, nurturing energy that supports your growth. Finally, approach this practice with openness and trust. At first, you may feel unsure or even skeptical, but remember: your energy responds to your attention. The more you give yourself permission to let go of what no longer serves you and welcome in supportive tools like crystals, the more you will notice tangible shifts, lighter moods, clearer thoughts, and a deeper sense of peace. This is not about superstition; it's about learning to work with energy in a way that empowers you, just as Anna discovered.

Anna's story is a perfect example of how these practices work in real life. When she first came to me, her home and her energy felt heavy and clouded, like she was carrying burdens that weren't hers. By beginning with a cleansing ritual, she was able to release the heavy, stagnant energy that had been clinging to her. Just as I described in the steps above, she started at her front door, worked her way through each room with sage, and intentionally set the direction for the energy she wanted to welcome in. That act alone gave her immediate relief, because she finally felt like she had the power to shift her environment rather than being a victim of it.

After her space was cleared, Anna incorporated crystals into her daily routine. She chose rose quartz to help rebuild self-love and black tourmaline for protection against outside negativity. Just as I suggested, she programmed her crystals with intentions that aligned with her needs, carried them in her pocket, and placed them in her bedroom to support restful sleep. Over time, she noticed that the drained, "vampire-sucked" feeling she had described began to fade. The consistency of these small steps brought her lasting energy, peace, and clarity.

The exact same steps that worked for Anna are available to you. Cleansing your space, choosing supportive crystals, and practicing consistently are not just abstract ideas; they are tangible actions that lead to real change. Her story shows you what's possible when you put these "how-tos" into practice: freedom from heaviness, protection from negativity, and a renewed sense of empowerment.

Just like Anna, you may be feeling weighed down by stress, negativity, or energy that doesn't even belong to you. This is where reclaiming your key begins by learning to clear what no longer serves you and aligning with tools that support your highest good. Cleansing rituals and the use of crystals are not about superstition; they are about creating space for clarity, healing, and renewed purpose. When you release stagnant energy and invite in supportive vibrations, you begin to reconnect with your inner self. The peace, balance, and empowerment you seek are not out of reach; they are waiting for you the moment you choose to take these small but powerful steps.

When you commit to cleansing your space and working with crystals, you open the door to transformation. These practices clear away the heaviness that blocks your energy and create an environment where peace and strength can thrive. As you take these steps, you'll notice that the chaos of life feels less overwhelming, your intuition grows stronger, and you begin to feel supported instead of drained. These are the very promises of this book to help you unlock your inner self, reclaim your power, and live with greater purpose and peace. Keep moving forward, and you'll discover that each action you take is guiding you closer to the life you've always desired.

Reflection Exercise: Clearing Space, Inviting Light

1. Choose a Space to Cleanse

Pick one area of your life that feels heavy: your bedroom, your car, or even your own energy. Take a moment to notice how the space feels before cleansing. Is it cluttered, stagnant, or draining?

2. Cleanse with Intention

Using sage, palo santo, and sound (like a bell or singing bowl), move through the space slowly. As you do, repeat silently or aloud, "I release all that no longer serves me. I invite in peace, clarity, and light."

3. Connect with a Crystal

Select a crystal that resonates with you, perhaps amethyst for calm, rose quartz for love, or clear quartz for clarity. Hold it in your hands, close your eyes, and set an intention:

"This crystal supports me in [state your desire i.e., "peace," "love," "balance," etc.]."

As you continue to cleanse your environment and align your energy with intention, you're preparing yourself for deeper spiritual work. Each act of clearing, grounding, and balancing opens space for higher awareness to emerge. The next step in your journey takes you beyond your physical surroundings and into the realm of light and consciousness itself—where your energy body becomes the bridge between earth and spirit. In the following chapter, you'll learn how meditation and the activation of your MerKaBa can expand your connection to the universe, awaken your higher potential, and guide you into profound states of peace and awareness.

Chapter 7:

Meditation and Activating Your MerKaBa

Key 6. Meditation and activating your MerKaBa: opening pathways to stillness and higher awareness

Years ago, I began seeing the numbers 12:12 everywhere on clocks, receipts, and license plates, etc., almost as if the universe itself were sending me a message. I couldn't help but wonder, why now? Why me? My curiosity led me to the MerKaBa, sometimes spelled Merkaba or Merkabah, and I was instantly captivated. I dove deep into learning; reading about it from every perspective I could find. What I discovered was astonishing: 12:12 is believed to be a code, a cosmic signal that your consciousness is awakening, preparing you to perceive beyond the physical world and step into your higher potential.

The MerKaBa is known as a "light body vehicle," a sacred tool that can support your ascension and divine potential. Its name alone holds profound meaning: Mer—Light, Ka—Spirit, Ba—Body. It is the union of spirit and body, surrounded and elevated by light. The symbol, formed by two interlocking tetrahedrons spinning in counter-rotating fields of energy, represents balance, protection, and alignment. There is so much more to the MerKaBa, but what captivated me most was the promise of personal transformation it offered.

I was determined to awaken mine. I began practicing specific MerKaBa meditations, yet the first attempts brought little more than anticipation. I soon realized that awakening this energy is deeply personal; what works for one soul may not awaken another. One quiet night, during a guided meditation, I felt a subtle activation stirring within me. Still, I longed for more. On the third attempt with a different activation, something extraordinary happened. The energy surged from my heart, enveloping me completely.

The true activation of my MerKaBa transformed me. Old beliefs, limitations, and fears melted away. I saw the world through a lens of love, clarity, and infinite possibility. I felt reborn, light, expansive, and deeply connected to all that is. I traveled through realms of consciousness, healed on physical and energetic levels, manifested intentions with ease, and connected with my guides and highest soul purpose. This sacred practice illuminated my path, showing me that the power, love, and wisdom we seek have always existed within us, waiting for the moment we choose to awaken them.

Around the same time that I was exploring these deeper spiritual truths, I also began to realize the importance of daily meditation. At first, I thought meditation was something you only did when you needed to relax or quiet your mind after a stressful day. But as I made it a consistent practice, I quickly learned it was so much more. Meditation became a daily reset for my soul, a way to clear away the noise of the outside world and reconnect with the still, powerful presence within. Even just ten minutes in the morning shifted the entire tone of my day. I felt calmer, clearer, and more grounded, able to move through challenges with more ease and grace instead of being consumed by them.

Over time, the practice began to open doors within me that I didn't even know existed. I received insights during meditation that helped me make difficult decisions, creative ideas seemed to flow with less effort, and I noticed I was more present in my relationships. Most importantly, meditation became a way to strengthen my connection with my Higher Self. The more I committed to showing up daily, even when I didn't feel like it, the more I experienced alignment, synchronicities, and inner peace. It was as though the universe was waiting for me to slow down long enough to listen. Daily meditation taught me that transformation doesn't always come through one big breakthrough but often through the quiet, consistent moments of choosing stillness and turning inward.

This story is a reminder that transformation is not only possible but also available to everyone. The practices of meditation and energetic activation aren't reserved for a chosen few; they are tools that anyone can learn and integrate into daily life. By seeing how my own journey unfolded, you can recognize that the peace, clarity, and connection I experienced are not unique to me; they are outcomes waiting for you as well. When you make space for meditation and begin consistently connecting with your higher self, you allow your inner wisdom to rise, your energy to align, and your life to shift in meaningful ways. What once felt overwhelming or out of reach becomes manageable and even miraculous.

Now I want to challenge you. What would your life look like if you gave yourself just ten or fifteen minutes each day to sit in stillness, breathe, and listen within? Could you release some of the noise, the distractions, and the constant pull of the outside world and begin reconnecting to your true self? The old way of pushing through stress, relying only on willpower, or ignoring your deeper needs hasn't given you the peace or fulfillment you long for. Meditation offers you a new way forward, one that restores balance, clarity, and strength from the inside out. The question is, Are you willing to begin?

Invitation Exercise: Daily Stillness Meditation

1. Find Your Space

Choose a quiet place where you won't be interrupted. Sit comfortably, either on a chair with your feet flat on the ground or cross-legged on a cushion. Rest your hands gently in your lap.

2. Breathe Deeply

Close your eyes and take three slow, deep breaths. Inhale through your nose, filling your lungs completely. Exhale through your mouth, releasing any tension. With each breath, feel your body soften, and your mind begin to settle.

3. Set Your Intention

Silently say to yourself, "I allow myself to release distractions and connect with my higher self." Let this intention guide your meditation.

4. Focus on the Heart

Bring your awareness to the center of your chest, your heart space. Imagine a soft light glowing there, growing brighter with each breath. This is your inner light, always present, always guiding you.

5. Release and Receive

As thoughts arise, acknowledge them without judgment and gently return your focus to your breath and the light in your heart. Allow yourself to simply be in the stillness.

6. Close with Gratitude

After 10–15 minutes, take a final deep breath and thank yourself for creating this time. Slowly open your eyes and carry this calm, centered energy into the rest of your day.

Bill came to me feeling consumed by life's demands. He described his mind as a constant storm of racing thoughts, work deadlines, family responsibilities, and the weight of expectations pulling him in every direction. Even when he tried to rest, he couldn't quiet the chatter. He admitted he had never really taken time to slow down, let alone meditate. His nervous system was exhausted, and his spirit longed for peace, though he didn't know how to find it.

During our sessions, I introduced Bill to the practice of simple daily meditation. At first, he doubted himself. "I can't sit still; my mind just won't stop," he told me. But I reassured him that meditation isn't about forcing silence; it's about creating space to listen inward. We began with just five minutes of focusing on his breath and heart space each morning. Slowly, something shifted. After a few weeks, he began noticing moments of calm throughout his day. He started handling challenges with more clarity, and the stress that once consumed him felt lighter. Bill told me, "It feels like I've finally found a place inside myself that I can return to no matter what's going on around me." Meditation had become his anchor, his way of reconnecting with his Higher Self and releasing the chaos that once ruled his life.

Bill's story shows us that meditation isn't reserved for monks or those who live in silence; it's a tool for anyone, especially in our fast-paced world. What made the difference for him was not perfection, but consistency and willingness. The same is true for you. To experience the benefits, you don't need to meditate for hours a day or "empty your mind" completely. What you do need is the attitude of openness, the skill of returning to your breath or your heart when distractions arise, and the commitment to show up for yourself daily, even if it's just for five minutes. By starting small and staying consistent, you'll notice moments of peace, clarity, and connection that ripple into every area of your life. Meditation is less about "doing it right" and more about allowing yourself to be present. If you adopt this practice with patience and self-compassion, you too will discover the calm, clarity, and inner strength that Bill found waiting within himself.

Invitation Exercise: Your First Step Into Stillness

Find a quiet space where you won't be disturbed. Sit comfortably with your feet planted on the ground, close your eyes, and take three deep, slow breaths. Place one hand on your heart and the other on your belly. As you breathe in, silently say to yourself, "I am here." As you breathe out, silently say, "I release." Do this for just five minutes. If your mind wanders, gently bring it back to your breath and your heart. When you're done, notice how you feel lighter, calmer, or perhaps simply more aware. This simple practice is how you begin building the bridge to your Higher Self, just as Bill did.

Grounding Exercise: Rooting Into the Earth

Step outside if you can or simply sit near a window with natural light. Remove your shoes and place your feet flat on the ground. Close your eyes and take slow, steady breaths. Imagine roots extending from the soles of your feet, traveling deep into the earth. With every exhale, let go of stress, tension, and heavy energy, sending it down through the roots. With every inhale, feel the nurturing energy of the earth rising to fill you with stability, calm, and strength. Stay with this visualization for 5–10 minutes. When you open your eyes, notice how much more present and centered you feel.

MerKaBa Activation Practice: Beginning the Journey

Find a quiet, comfortable place where you can sit without distraction. Close your eyes and begin with slow, steady breathing. Visualize a brilliant light in the center of your heart, glowing brighter with each inhale. As you breathe, imagine two interlocking tetrahedrons of light forming around your body, one pointing upward (Father Sky energy) rotating clockwise and one pointing downward (Mother Earth energy) rotating counterclockwise. With every breath, see them begin to rotate in opposite directions, creating a protective, radiant field of light around you. Even if you don't feel the full activation yet, simply holding this visualization begins to align your energy and awaken your light body. Stay with the practice for 10–15 minutes, and when you finish, notice any shifts in clarity, peace, or energy.

The practices and steps outlined above, daily meditation, grounding exercises, and MerKaBa activation, directly mirror the transformations Bill and I experienced together. Just as Bill began with five minutes of daily meditation and gradually reclaimed his calm and clarity, you too can use these techniques to release overwhelm and reconnect with your Higher Self.

Grounding exercises, such as visualizing roots into the earth, anchor your energy and create stability in the midst of life's chaos, much like my own experience learning to connect with Mother Earth and Father Sky. MerKaBa meditations allow you to expand your consciousness and activate your inner light, just as I did when I felt my heart open and old patterns dissolve.

By consistently applying these steps, you create a practical framework for aligning your mind, body, and spirit, turning abstract concepts into tangible results. The stories you've read are proof: when you show up and apply these practices, transformation isn't just possible, it becomes inevitable.

Now it's your turn. Take these practices—daily meditation, grounding, and MerKaBa activation—and weave them into your own life. Start small: commit to five minutes of meditation each morning, visualize your roots grounding into the earth for stability, and explore a short MerKaBa activation to expand your energy. Notice how your awareness, clarity, and inner strength begin to shift as you practice consistently. These steps are not just exercises; they are the keys to reclaiming your power, aligning with your purpose, and experiencing the peace that has always been within you. Just as Bill and I experienced transformation through these practices, you too can unlock your inner self and step fully into the life you were meant to live.

By embracing these practices—daily meditation, grounding, and MerKaBa activation—you are opening the door to profound transformation. The peace, clarity, and alignment you've been seeking are not distant goals; they are already within you, waiting for your attention and action. As you commit to these steps, you will begin to release old patterns, restore your energy, and reconnect with your Higher Self. Just like Bill, you can experience calm amidst chaos, clarity amidst confusion, and a renewed sense of purpose in every area of your life. Keep practicing, stay consistent, and trust the process—your power, your purpose, and your peace are unfolding right now, one intentional step at a time.

As your meditation deepens and your MerKaBa begins to awaken, you'll find yourself more attuned to the subtle language of energy—the vibrations that flow through and around all living things. This growing awareness naturally leads to the next step in your journey: understanding and balancing the energetic centers within your body. Just as meditation harmonizes your mind and spirit, chakra work harmonizes your entire being. In the next chapter, we'll explore the power of chakras and Reiki, two practices that help you channel healing energy, restore balance, and align your physical, emotional, and spiritual systems, allowing your inner light to flow freely once again.

Chapter 8:

Chakra Balancing and Reiki

Key 7. Energy healing practices: these
include chakra balancing, Reiki, shamanic
work, and self-hypnosis: restoring flow,
harmony, and wholeness

In 2017, shortly after my mother was diagnosed with breast cancer, my entire perspective on healing began to shift. Watching her navigate such a difficult journey stirred something deep within me. I felt called to search for alternative methods of rejuvenation and support, not only for her but for myself as well. That's when I first discovered Reiki. The more I read about it, the more fascinated I became. It was as though every page I turned, every story I uncovered, was speaking directly to my soul. My curiosity quickly grew into passion, and before I knew it, I was driving all the way from Arizona to California to study under a magnificent Reiki instructor. That trip changed my life.

I enrolled in Usui Reiki Level 1, a class filled with wisdom, energy, and ancient practices that resonated with me so deeply. It wasn't just information; it felt like remembering something I had always known. Alongside Reiki, I also began exploring chakra balancing, and when I started incorporating these techniques into my own life and later with clients, the results were astonishing. To see people light up with more energy, balance, and peace was nothing short of magical. That was the moment I knew I couldn't stop there. My heart was set on continuing this journey, and eventually, I became a Reiki Master. In Level 1, we focused primarily on the seven main chakras: the root, sacral, solar plexus, heart, throat, third eye, and crown. But as I advanced, I began working with the expanded twelve-chakra system, and activating these higher energy centers left me truly in awe. It opened doors to levels of healing and consciousness I had never experienced before, and I knew I had stepped onto a lifelong path of energy work and spiritual discovery.

Healing and transformation often begin with curiosity and the willingness to explore new paths. Just as I discovered Reiki and chakra balancing during one of the most difficult times in my life, you too can begin incorporating these practices to support your own well-being. Reiki and chakra work are not just about energy; they are about creating harmony, balance, and alignment within yourself so you can navigate life's challenges with strength and clarity. By opening yourself to these tools, you give your body, mind, and spirit the opportunity to release what no longer serves you and to awaken to deeper levels of peace and vitality. My journey illustrates that the answers we seek are often closer than we think, and by taking that first step, you can begin experiencing profound shifts in your own life.

Have you ever stopped to wonder if the way you've been living is serving you or simply draining you? So many people go through life carrying stress, imbalance, and exhaustion, convincing themselves that it's "just the way life is." But let me challenge you: what if that belief is the very thing keeping you stuck? What if the old way, the endless cycle of pushing through, ignoring your needs, and hoping things will change on their own, is not only failing you but also costing you your peace, health, and joy? If you've felt disconnected, heavy, or out of alignment, it's not a sign of weakness; it's a sign your energy system is calling for attention.

Now, imagine a different way. Instead of letting an imbalance control you, what if you chose to actively create harmony within your body, mind, and spirit? Tools like Reiki and chakra balancing are not abstract ideas; they are practical pathways to release stagnant energy, restore balance, and reconnect you with your highest potential. This is your invitation to stop settling for survival and start stepping into true healing and alignment. The direction is clear: the old way of ignoring your inner world will keep you stuck, but a new path of energy work and self-care can open the door to freedom, peace, and transformation. The question is, are you ready to step through it?

Lisa came to me at a time when her life felt completely out of balance. She described feeling like she was running on empty, juggling work, family, and constant obligations with no energy left for herself. She admitted she hadn't even thought about self-care in years because she believed everyone else's needs had to come first. By the time she reached out, Lisa was experiencing chronic fatigue, anxiety, and a deep sense of disconnection from herself. She told me, "I feel like I'm living on autopilot, and I

71

don't even recognize myself anymore." During our Reiki and chakra balancing sessions, we gently began to release the layers of stagnant energy that had built up over time. As her chakras realigned, Lisa described feeling lighter, clearer, and more grounded. She started noticing subtle shifts in her daily life: her anxiety softened, her sleep improved, and her ability to set boundaries grew stronger. Most importantly, she felt reconnected to her own energy and inner guidance. "I feel like I have myself back," she said after just a few sessions. Her story is proof that when you choose to stop ignoring your inner world and step into practices that nurture your energy, true transformation begins.

Lisa's transformation didn't happen by chance. It came from intentional steps that you, too, can begin to take. Here's how you can start applying these practices in your own life:

1. Acknowledge your imbalance. Just as Lisa admitted she was on autopilot, the first step is honesty with yourself. Where are you running on empty? Where do you feel disconnected or overwhelmed? Awareness is the doorway to change.

2. Cleanse your energy. Energy builds up, sometimes heavy, stagnant, or overwhelming. Practices like Reiki, chakra balancing, smudging with sage, or even simple breathwork help clear away what no longer serves you. This allows fresh, vibrant energy to flow freely again.

3. Balance your chakras. Each chakra represents an aspect of your physical, emotional, and spiritual self. When one is blocked or overactive, an imbalance follows. Visualization, meditation, sound healing, or energy sessions can restore harmony, creating a foundation for clarity, vitality, and peace.

4. Reconnect to your inner guidance. As Lisa experienced, when her energy centers opened and aligned, her intuition grew stronger. This connection is already within you—you just need to quiet the noise and tune in. Daily stillness, journaling, or guided meditations can support this process.

5. Commit to ongoing self-care. Energy work isn't a one-time fix; it's a lifestyle shift. Incorporating regular practices, whether professional sessions or your own routines, ensures you maintain balance, resilience, and alignment.

When you follow these steps, you begin to experience the same freedom and reconnection Lisa did. It's not about quick fixes. It's about choosing a new path of harmony.

Chapter Challenge: Realigning Your Energy

1. Reflection Questions

1) Where in your life do you feel the most "out of balance" right now, physically, emotionally, or spiritually?
2) When was the last time you truly felt clear, energized, and connected to yourself? What was different about that moment?
3) Which chakra (root, sacral, solar plexus, heart, throat, third eye, or crown) do you suspect may need the most attention? Trust your intuition.
4) What is one expectation, habit, or relationship that feels heavy or is draining your energy?

2. Your Challenge

This week, choose one practice to begin shifting your energy:

- Commit to a 5-minute daily meditation where you focus on breathing light into your body and exhaling stress.

- Light a candle, burn sage, or use sound (a bell or singing bowl) to cleanse your space and notice how the energy feels afterward.
- Place a crystal on your heart or solar plexus during rest, setting the intention to release old patterns and invite balance.
- Journal each day about how your body feels when you give yourself space to reset.

Remember: you don't have to do everything at once. Start small, stay consistent, and let your energy shift little by little. Over time, these practices open the door to the peace, clarity, and vitality you've been searching for.

Just like Lisa's story revealed how energy healing helped her release years of imbalance, the steps I've outlined above are here to guide you on the same path. When you take time to meditate, cleanse your space, or use crystals with intention, you are actively doing what Lisa did: releasing the heaviness, restoring flow, and inviting in peace. These practices are not abstract; they are real, tangible tools that create shifts you can feel in your body, mind, and spirit. Every time you commit to even one small step, you are choosing to move from being stuck in survival mode to stepping into alignment and freedom. Lisa found her breakthrough by incorporating these tools into her daily life, and the same possibility is available for you.

If you've been longing for clarity, peace, and a deeper sense of purpose, this is your chance to apply what you've just learned to your own life. *The key to you* has always been within you; you only need the tools to unlock it. By practicing self-care, grounding, meditation, Reiki, or chakra balancing, you are giving yourself permission to heal at the root level instead of covering up the symptoms. These practices meet you where you are, addressing the stress, imbalance, or disconnection you've been carrying, and guiding you toward the peace, alignment, and purpose you deserve. This is not about temporary fixes; it's about reclaiming your key and finally stepping into the life your soul has been waiting for.

When you begin to apply these steps, you'll notice the promises of this journey unfolding: greater balance in your daily life, deeper clarity in your decisions, and a renewed sense of energy and peace. These tools aren't just practices; they are pathways back to your true self, helping you release what no longer serves you and align with what your soul has been calling for. By taking consistent action, even in small ways, you'll move from merely surviving to fully thriving, manifesting the love, abundance, and purpose that have always been within your reach. This is the fulfillment of *the key to you*, and it all begins with your choice to unlock it.

As you continue along this path of energetic healing, you'll begin to realize that Reiki and chakra balancing are only the beginning. Once your energy starts to flow freely again, deeper layers of transformation become accessible—layers connected not just to your present life but to your ancestral roots and spiritual lineage. The next step on this journey invites you to explore the ancient wisdom of shamanic healing, where energy work meets the soul's oldest memories. This is where true, soul-level restoration begins—where you reconnect with the parts of yourself that have long awaited integration and wholeness.

Chapter 9:

Shamanic Healing

Key 7. Energy healing practices: these include chakra balancing, Reiki, shamanic work, and self-hypnosis: restoring flow, harmony, and wholeness

---

In the early days of my spiritual journey, I never imagined I would be called to shamanic practices. At the time, I was simply searching for deeper answers, something beyond the surface-level solutions that never seemed to last. I felt a pull, almost like a whisper from within, guiding me toward ancient wisdom and practices that connected directly to the soul. My first experience with shamanic healing was both humbling and transformative. I remember sitting quietly, unsure of what to expect, when I felt the presence of something greater, an energy that seemed to reach into places within me I didn't even know needed healing. The session revealed old wounds, unprocessed emotions, and ancestral patterns I had been unconsciously carrying. It was as if a door had opened, and I was finally able to see that true healing required going beneath the surface, to the very root of the soul.

That first encounter left such an impression on me that I couldn't ignore it. I felt a fire ignite inside of me, a deep curiosity to learn more about the sacred practices of shamanism. I began reading, studying, and seeking teachers who could guide me on this path. The more I learned, the more I realized how powerful and necessary these practices were, not just for me but for anyone longing for true healing and reconnection to their soul. I felt a deep responsibility to not only experience this work but to understand it so I could eventually share it with others.

Over the years, my passion for shamanism led me to pursue multiple certifications, each deepening my connection and knowledge. I became a certified Shamanic Life Coach, helping others uncover the root causes of their struggles and guiding them through their healing journeys. I trained as a certified Earth Medicine Practitioner, learning to work with the elements and the wisdom of nature in profound and restorative ways. Eventually, I earned the title of certified Master of Shamanism, a path that required dedication, humility, and a commitment to walking this sacred road with integrity.

Looking back, I see how this journey transformed me in ways I could have never predicted. What began as a search for personal healing became a lifelong calling to guide others in reclaiming their power, healing their wounds, and reconnecting with the ancient wisdom that still lives within us all. Shamanism taught me that we are never truly broken; we are simply waiting to be remembered, restored, and realigned with our true essence.

My story is meant to show you that shamanic practices are not just mystical or reserved for a chosen few; they are accessible, practical, and deeply transformative tools available to anyone ready to heal at the soul level. Like me, you may be carrying wounds, patterns, or energy that keep you feeling stuck and disconnected, even if you've tried other methods of healing before.

Shamanic work goes beyond surface-level fixes by addressing the root causes of imbalance, often hidden in the subconscious, the body, or even ancestral memory. By opening yourself to these practices, you too can release what no longer serves you, reconnect with your inner wisdom, and reclaim the power needed to live your purpose with confidence and peace. My journey is proof that with openness and willingness, you can step into this same level of healing and transformation.

Have you ever felt like no matter how much you try to "fix" yourself on the outside, something still feels unsettled deep within? Maybe you've changed jobs, relationships, or routines, only to find the same patterns and struggles creeping back into your life. That's because true healing doesn't come from surface-level changes; it comes from going inward, to the very root of the wound. The old way of pushing through, numbing, or distracting yourself may have helped you survive, but it will never allow you to truly thrive. If you keep ignoring the deeper call of your soul, the cycles of exhaustion, disconnection, and emptiness will only repeat. The truth is that your inner world cannot be healed by avoiding it—it can only be transformed by facing it with courage and guidance.

This is where shamanic practices step in as a new direction. Instead of continuing down the path of quick fixes and temporary relief, what if you chose to step into a journey of lasting healing and reconnection? Shamanic tools, like soul retrievals, earth medicine, and deep energy clearing, help uncover what's been hidden, release what no longer belongs, and bring back the parts of you that have been lost along the way. It's not always the easiest path; it requires honesty, openness, and a willingness to let go of old ways of being, but it is the most rewarding. Imagine living with more clarity, strength, and alignment than ever before. The invitation is here: will you keep repeating the same cycles, or are you ready to step into a deeper truth and unlock the healing your soul has been waiting for?

Emily came to me after years of feeling like something in her life was missing. On the outside, she seemed to have it all together: a stable job, a busy social life, and a calendar full of responsibilities. But inside, she admitted she felt hollow, disconnected, and tired of repeating the same cycles of stress and burnout. She described it as "stuck in a rut," where no matter what she accomplished, the emptiness always returned. During our first shamanic healing session, I could sense the heaviness she was carrying: old wounds, unresolved grief, and the weight of expectations that weren't truly hers. Her energy felt fragmented, like pieces of herself had been left behind over the years.

Through soul retrieval and guided shamanic practices, Emily began to reconnect with those lost parts of herself. It was as if pieces of her soul were returning home. She shared how, for the first time in years, she felt whole again.

She started noticing subtle but profound changes. Her anxiety eased, her intuition became stronger, and her relationships shifted into greater harmony. Most importantly, she felt aligned with her true self, no longer forcing her life to fit into roles that drained her. Emily's story is a reminder that deep healing requires more than surface changes; it calls for courage to look inward and reclaim the parts of yourself that have been hidden or forgotten. And when you do, the transformation is powerful: peace, clarity, and the freedom to finally live as your authentic self.

To experience the kind of transformation Emily did, you must first be willing to look honestly at yourself and acknowledge where you are right now. This takes courage because it means admitting that the way you've been living is no longer serving you. Ask yourself, "Am I truly happy, or am I just getting through the days? Do I feel connected to my purpose, or do I feel like I'm drifting without direction?"

The first skill you must develop is awareness. Without awareness, nothing changes. By slowing down, tuning into your feelings, and observing your patterns, you begin to identify where your energy has become blocked or fragmented.

The next step is cultivating an attitude of openness. Shamanic practices, energy work, and spiritual healing require you to release rigid expectations and trust that the process may look different than what your logical mind imagines. Healing isn't always linear; it can feel like peeling back layers of yourself. This is why being open and patient with yourself is so essential. Openness allows you to explore practices like grounding rituals, soul retrieval, or guided meditations without judgment, giving them space to work their way into your life and bring you the shifts you desire.

Another critical action is commitment. Transformation does not happen overnight; it comes from consistent practices that nourish your soul and help you realign with your truth. Whether it's a daily grounding exercise, regular meditation, or intentional time spent in nature, these small, steady actions build momentum. Just like Emily, you may not notice the changes immediately, but over time, you'll begin to feel lighter, more centered, and more connected.

Finally, you must cultivate self-compassion. Healing often stirs up emotions, memories, or patterns that you've carried for years. Instead of judging yourself or pushing the discomfort away, meet yourself with kindness. See these moments as opportunities to grow, not setbacks. The attitude of compassion ensures that when challenges arise, you don't abandon the process; you lean into it. And that's when the breakthroughs happen.

When you embrace awareness, openness, commitment, and compassion, you create the foundation for lasting transformation. These qualities, paired with the practices I share in this book, will guide you to release old wounds, reclaim lost energy, and reconnect with the essence of who you truly are. This is the path forward, and it's available to you the moment you choose to begin.

Think back to Emily's story. When she first came to me, she was struggling under the weight of expectations, disconnected from herself, drained by the weight of expectations, and unsure of what direction to take. What began to shift everything for her was the very first step I outlined: awareness. She admitted that the way she was living wasn't working, and that honesty opened the door for her healing journey. Once she allowed herself to become aware of the truth, we were able to work together to identify the blockages and begin the process of release.

Her next breakthrough came when she embraced openness. At first, she was skeptical of shamanic practices. She wondered how something so different from her usual way of thinking could help. But the moment she chose to release her doubt and lean into the experience, the healing began to unfold. This mirrors the journey you, too, can take. Without openness, the wisdom and tools available to you will remain untouched.

Emily also showed great commitment. She didn't just try one session and walk away. She kept showing up for herself, practicing the grounding rituals we discussed, journaling her insights, and returning for further healing. Over time, these practices created lasting change in her energy and outlook. This is the same consistency you will need to apply if you want to experience deep, sustainable transformation.

And perhaps most importantly, Emily learned self-compassion. Healing stirred up old wounds and difficult emotions for her, and at times she felt frustrated. But instead of giving up, she met herself with gentleness. That shift allowed her to integrate her experiences instead of resisting them. The compassion she developed became the very key that unlocked her freedom.

Just like Emily, your path will be shaped by these four steps: awareness, openness, commitment, and compassion. Together, they form the bridge between where you are now and the life of clarity, peace, and purpose you are seeking. The stories I've shared are living proof that these practices work.

1. Awareness Exercise – Energy Check-In

Take a quiet moment at the beginning and end of your day. Place your hand over your heart, close your eyes, and ask yourself, "Where am I holding tension? What emotions are present in me right now?" Without judgment, simply notice what arises. This daily check-in helps you become aware of your energy and emotional state, allowing you to see patterns you may not otherwise recognize.

2. Openness Exercise – Journaling with Curiosity

Set aside ten minutes to write freely about something you're struggling with or questioning in your life. Instead of focusing on solutions, approach it with curiosity. Take a few moments to write your reflections on these questions: "What if I looked at this differently? What might I learn from this experience?" This shifts your mind from resistance to openness, creating space for new insights.

3. Commitment Exercise – Grounding Ritual

Choose one grounding practice, such as walking barefoot outside, sitting with your back against a tree, or visualizing roots growing from your feet deep into the Earth. Commit to doing this every day for one week, even if only for a few minutes. The key here is not how long you do it, but that you show up consistently. This daily act will strengthen your energetic foundation.

4. Compassion Exercise – Loving-Kindness Meditation

Close your eyes, breathe deeply, and silently repeat, "May I be safe. May I be at peace. May I be free from suffering. May I live with ease." After a few rounds, extend this blessing to others: loved ones, strangers, and even those who challenge you. This practice softens self-judgment and nurtures compassion for both yourself and others.

Each of these exercises ties back to the stories I've shared; they are the very tools my clients have used to shift their energy, release blockages, and begin walking their path of healing. If you practice them with intention, you'll start to notice the subtle yet powerful ways they create transformation in your own life.

These exercises are not just spiritual "add-ons," they are practical doorways into the very transformation you desire. If your heart longs for balance, healing, and a deeper connection to your Higher Self, then practicing awareness, openness, commitment, and compassion in daily, tangible ways will guide you there.

Think of it as building an energetic foundation: by checking in with yourself, opening your perspective, committing to grounding rituals, and cultivating compassion, you are aligning your inner world with the harmony you've been seeking. This is how you move from merely surviving to truly thriving, from feeling disconnected to stepping into the wholeness and purpose you were meant to embody.

When you begin to take these small but powerful steps, you will discover that healing and transformation are not distant dreams but living realities within your reach. By grounding your energy, opening to new awareness, and nurturing compassion for yourself, you invite balance, clarity, and strength into your daily life. These practices are the keys to unlocking peace, vitality, and alignment with your highest purpose. The promise is simple yet profound: when you choose this path, you will no longer feel held down by the old cycles that once held you back. Instead, you will step into a life filled with light, freedom, and the deep knowing that you are whole, supported, and capable of living your true potential.

Just as shamanic healing helps you uncover and restore the hidden parts of your soul, the next step on your journey takes you even deeper—into the landscape of your own mind. The subconscious holds powerful patterns, memories, and beliefs that shape how you experience the world. While shamanic work reconnects you with your spirit, hypnosis opens the doorway to your inner programming, allowing you to rewrite the stories that no longer serve you. In the following chapter, you'll learn how hypnosis and self-hypnosis can help you quiet the noise of doubt, release fear at its root, and awaken the confident, calm, and empowered version of yourself that's been waiting within.

Chapter 10:

Hypnosis and Self-Hypnosis

Key 7. Energy healing practices: these include chakra balancing, Reiki, shamanic work, and self-hypnosis: restoring flow, harmony, and wholeness

---

Years ago, I found myself struggling with persistent anxiety and self-doubt. No matter how many strategies I tried—meditation, grounding, and even energy healing—there were moments when fear and stress would creep in, seemingly out of nowhere. I knew there had to be a deeper, more direct way to reach my subconscious mind and release the patterns that were keeping me stuck. That's when I discovered hypnosis, and I engaged in multiple sessions with a hypnotherapist at the time, which helped me tremendously. After these sessions, as instructed by my hypnotherapist, I included the power of self-hypnosis.

At first, I was hesitant. The idea of guiding myself into a trance seemed unfamiliar and even a little intimidating. But I committed to learning, practicing, and understanding the process. During my first self-hypnosis session, I remember the incredible sense of calm that washed over me as I focused inward, letting go of tension and negative thought loops. It was as if I had entered a quiet sanctuary within my own mind, one that had always been there but that I had never truly accessed. In that space, I could reprogram my thoughts, reinforce positive beliefs, and release fears that had been quietly controlling my decisions.

Over time, I practiced consistently. Each session allowed me to dig a little deeper, uncover old patterns, and replace them with empowering truths. I began noticing how quickly I could shift from stress to calm, from doubt to confidence. The most profound change wasn't just in how I felt; it was in how I responded to life. I became more centered, resilient, and in control of my choices. Hypnosis and self-hypnosis gave me a tool to access my inner mind, heal from within, and step into a life aligned with my true self.

This experience taught me that the answers we seek are often already inside us; we just need a method to access them. Hypnosis is that method. It offers a direct pathway to the subconscious, where old beliefs and patterns live, allowing you to release what no longer serves you and install the intentions and habits that will help you thrive. By learning and practicing this skill, you too can unlock the inner peace, confidence, and clarity that have always been available to you.

This story demonstrates that the key to lasting change often lies in accessing the subconscious mind, the place where beliefs, habits, and emotional patterns are stored. By sharing my own journey with hypnosis and self-hypnosis, you will see that transformation is possible, even when traditional methods feel insufficient. Whether you choose to work with a skilled hypnotherapist or practice self-hypnosis on your own, the principle remains the same: consistent, intentional engagement with your inner mind allows you to release limiting patterns, reinforce empowering beliefs, and step fully into your true potential. This story provides a roadmap, showing that the solution is not abstract; it is practical, accessible, and designed to create tangible results in your life.

One of the most powerful lessons I've learned on this journey comes from the idea that true change begins within. As Napoleon Hill famously wrote, "Knowledge has no value except that which can be gained from its application toward some worthy end." This perfectly captures the essence of hypnosis and self-hypnosis: understanding the theory is not enough; you must take intentional action to apply it. By consistently engaging with your subconscious mind, whether through guided sessions or self-practice, you begin to release old patterns, reframe limiting beliefs, and align your thoughts, emotions, and behaviors with the life you truly desire. This principle has been a guiding light in my own path and has informed every technique and approach I share with my clients.

My goal in sharing these tools and experiences with you is simple: I want to empower you to reclaim your inner strength, clarity, and peace. I want you to see that the answers you've been searching for are already within you and that with the right techniques like hypnosis, self-hypnosis, and conscious inner work, you can release what no longer serves you and step fully into your true potential. My intention is to guide you, support you, and show you a path that allows you to heal, transform, and create a life aligned with your highest purpose. Ultimately, my goal is for you to feel confident that you are your own key, capable of unlocking the life you've always desired.

Take a moment and look honestly inside yourself. Are there patterns, fears, or beliefs that have been quietly controlling your life? Have you tried the "old ways" of pushing through stress, ignoring discomfort, or hoping things will magically change, only to find yourself stuck in the same cycles? The truth is, the old way isn't working. It never has. It's keeping you trapped in habits and thought patterns that no longer serve your growth or happiness.

Lesley came to me feeling completely stuck. She described a life caught in anxiety, self-doubt, and recurring patterns that kept sabotaging her relationships and career. She had tried everything: therapy, meditation, even journaling, but nothing seemed to provide lasting change. During our first session, I introduced her to hypnosis as a tool to access her subconscious mind, where these limiting beliefs had taken root.

At first, Lesley was skeptical, unsure if she could even relax enough to let it work. But as we began, she felt a surprising sense of calm, like a heavy fog lifting. Through guided hypnosis, she was able to uncover the root of a recurring fear that had been influencing her decisions for years. Over several sessions, she learned to release this fear, replace it with empowering beliefs, and create new mental patterns aligned with her goals.

The transformation was remarkable. Lesley reported feeling lighter, more confident, and able to make choices she had previously avoided. She noticed changes in her career, relationships, and overall sense of self-worth. Her story illustrates the power of accessing the subconscious: by addressing the source of our challenges at their deepest level, we can create real, lasting change. This is exactly the solution I am proposing. Hypnosis and self-hypnosis are practical tools that allow you to unlock your inner potential and finally step into the life you've been longing for.

To benefit from what Lesley experienced, you must be willing to take intentional action and commit to consistent practice. First, cultivate the skill of self-awareness by noticing the recurring thoughts, fears, and patterns that influence your decisions and behaviors. Then, adopt the attitude of openness and trust: trust in the process, in your subconscious mind, and in your ability to create change.

Incorporating hypnosis or self-hypnosis is a practical step, but the true power comes from applying these techniques regularly, with focus and intention. Set aside time each day to practice, reflect, and reinforce new, empowering beliefs. By doing this, you begin to reprogram your subconscious, release limiting patterns, and align your mind, emotions, and actions with the life you truly desire. Transformation doesn't happen passively; it happens when you actively engage with the tools and techniques available to you.

Here are some effective techniques you can use to practice self-hypnosis and start accessing your subconscious mind:

1. Deep Breathing and Relaxation

Begin by finding a quiet, comfortable space. Close your eyes and take slow, deep breaths, inhaling through your nose and exhaling through your mouth. Focus on relaxing each part of your body, from your head down to your toes. This deep relaxation signals your mind that it's safe to enter a receptive state.

2. Visualization

Once relaxed, visualize a peaceful, safe place, a beach, forest, or garden. Imagine yourself fully immersed in this environment, noticing the sights, sounds, and sensations. This helps your mind shift into a calm, focused state where suggestions are more easily absorbed.

3. Positive Affirmations

While in this relaxed state, repeat empowering statements or affirmations that reflect the change you want. For example: "I am confident and capable," or "I release fear and embrace abundance." Speak them slowly and imagine them embedding into your subconscious.

4. Guided Self-Hypnosis Scripts

You can record your own script or use a pre-recorded one. Begin with relaxation cues, then guide yourself through visualizations and affirmations that target your specific goals. Listening regularly strengthens your subconscious rewiring.

5. Counting Technique

Start by counting down slowly from 10 to 1 with each breath, imagining yourself sinking deeper into relaxation with every number. Once you reach 1, you are in a receptive hypnotic state where positive suggestions and visualizations can be applied.

6. Anchoring

Choose a simple physical action, like pressing your thumb and forefinger together, while in your relaxed hypnotic state. Pair it with a positive affirmation. Over time, performing this action can trigger the calm, focused state instantly.

Consistency is key. Practicing even 10–15 minutes a day can help reprogram limiting beliefs, release old patterns, and align your mind with your desired reality.

10-Minute Self-Hypnosis Routine

Step 1: Find Your Space (1 min.)

Sit or lie down in a quiet, comfortable space where you won't be disturbed. Close your eyes and allow your body to settle.

Step 2: Deep Breathing (2 min.)

Take slow, deep breaths. Inhale through your nose for a count of 4, hold for 2, and exhale through your mouth for a count of 6. With each exhale, imagine tension leaving your body.

Step 3: Progressive Relaxation (2 min.)

Focus on relaxing your body from head to toe. Start with your scalp, jaw, and shoulders, and work down to your legs and feet. Imagine each muscle softening and releasing.

Step 4: Guided Visualization (2 min.)

Picture a peaceful, safe place where you feel completely calm and secure. Imagine the sights, sounds, and sensations around you. Immerse yourself fully in this environment.

Step 5: Positive Affirmations (2 min.)

Repeat affirmations aligned with your goals. For example:

- "I am confident and capable."
- "I release fear and embrace abundance."
- "I am in control of my thoughts, my choices, and my life."

Say each slowly, imagining it sinking deeply into your subconscious.

Step 6: Anchoring (1 min.)

Choose a simple physical action such as pressing your thumb and forefinger together. As you do this, feel the calm and focus of your hypnotic state embedding in your mind. Over time, this action will trigger relaxation and alignment instantly.

Step 7: Gradual Return (10 sec.)

Count slowly from 1 to 5, telling yourself that with each number you are becoming more alert, bringing back calm, focus, and clarity with you. Open your eyes and take a deep, grounding breath.

Tip: Practice daily for at least 10–15 minutes. Consistency rewires your subconscious, helping you release limiting patterns and strengthen empowering beliefs.

In Lesley's story, she struggled with deep-seated fears and limiting beliefs that had shaped her choices for years. By using hypnosis, she accessed her subconscious mind and uncovered the root of these patterns. The steps outlined above—deep breathing, progressive relaxation, visualization, affirmations, and anchoring—mirror the process she experienced in her sessions. Each step is designed to guide you into a receptive state, just as Lesley became receptive to uncovering and releasing her fears. The anchoring technique gives a practical tool to sustain that calm and clarity throughout daily life.

Finally, relating to your own story of awakening with hypnosis, the steps provided offer a blueprint to replicate the same process: entering a relaxed state, connecting with inner guidance, and replacing old mental patterns with empowering beliefs. Just as you experienced transformation through repeated practice, the routine allows you to take intentional action daily by accessing the subconscious mind and applying these tools. They can unlock their inner self, release limiting patterns, and step into a life of clarity, purpose, and peace.

By consistently practicing the steps outlined above, you are taking deliberate action toward reclaiming your inner power and transforming your life. Just as Lesley uncovered and released her fears, and my own journey with hypnosis revealed new levels of clarity and alignment, these tools are designed to guide you to the same breakthroughs. The promise of this work is real: by committing to these practices, you will begin to release limiting patterns, reconnect with your inner self, and step into a life filled with confidence, peace, and purpose. The transformation is within your reach, and with each small step, you are moving closer to living the empowered, fulfilled life that has always been waiting for you.

Hypnosis and self-hypnosis remind us that transformation begins within—that every belief, habit, and emotional pattern can be reshaped once we access the subconscious mind. As you've learned, the process is both deeply personal and profoundly empowering. Yet, the true beauty of this work lies in seeing how it unfolds in real lives. Each person's story becomes a mirror, showing us that healing takes many forms but always follows the same truth: when we turn inward with awareness and intention, change becomes inevitable. In the next chapter, you'll witness how these practices have touched the lives of others— real stories of healing, awakening, and transformation that will inspire your own journey forward.

Chapter 11:

Stories of Healing and Transformation

When you step back and reflect on everything we've explored, you can see how each piece connects into a unified path toward transformation. Whether it's grounding yourself, connecting with your Higher Self, cleansing your energy, practicing meditation, activating your MerKaBa, balancing your chakras, or using hypnosis, every tool offers its own unique benefit. Even taking action on just one of these tools can create noticeable shifts: increased clarity, renewed energy, or a sense of calm and purpose.

But when you begin to apply these practices together, holistically, the transformation becomes exponential. Each tool reinforces the others, working together in harmony to align your mind, body, and spirit. Grounding amplifies meditation, meditation deepens chakra work, and energy clearing enhances self-hypnosis. By committing to the full spectrum of practices, you open yourself to profound, lasting change, unlocking the life you've been seeking, fully aligned with your purpose, power, and peace.

Let's revisit the promises made in Chapter 1, as they are the foundation for everything you've learned and practiced since. In that chapter, I promised that by engaging with these tools and techniques, you would:

- Reclaim your inner power and personal authority.
- Release limiting beliefs and old patterns that no longer serve you.
- Restore balance, energy, and alignment within your mind, body, and spirit.
- Deepen your connection to your Higher Self and intuition.
- Experience greater peace, clarity, and confidence in your daily life.
- Step fully into your purpose, living with intention and fulfillment.

Each promise represents a tangible outcome, a shift you can feel and see in your life. The exercises, stories, and tools shared in the chapters since are designed to guide you directly toward these outcomes, providing a roadmap for transformation that is both practical and profound.

Lisa experienced a remarkable transformation after committing to the practices outlined in this book. When she first came to me, she felt completely disconnected from herself, stretched thin by work, family obligations, and self-doubt. After consistently applying grounding techniques, daily meditation, chakra balancing, and energy clearing, Lisa began noticing dramatic shifts. She felt calmer, more focused, and more in tune with her intuition. Her relationships improved because she was setting boundaries and honoring her own needs, and she found a renewed sense of purpose in her career.

Another example is my own journey with MerKaBa meditation and self-hypnosis. Initially, I struggled with mental clutter, anxiety, and a sense of being stuck in old patterns. By following the step-by-step techniques, daily meditations, energy activations, and self-reflection exercises, I experienced profound clarity and alignment. Old beliefs that had limited me for years began to dissolve, and I felt a deep connection to my Higher Self. Opportunities for growth, healing, and manifestation began appearing in ways I had never imagined.

These stories illustrate the power of applying these practices consistently. When you take action and integrate the tools and techniques presented throughout this book, the promises from Chapter 1—peace, clarity, purpose, and empowerment—become not just possibilities, but real, tangible outcomes in your life.

James provides a powerful example of what can happen when someone fully embraces these practices. When James first reached out to me, he was constantly exhausted and emotionally drained and felt trapped in a cycle of self-sabotage. He had tried countless quick-fix workshops, motivational books, and even therapy, but nothing seemed to stick. Together, we implemented a holistic approach using grounding exercises, energy clearing, chakra balancing, and guided meditations. At first, James found it challenging to stay consistent; old habits of overworking and people-pleasing kept pulling him back. But as he committed to the daily practices, subtle shifts began to appear. He noticed a newfound calm in stressful situations, a stronger sense of clarity when making decisions, and even a boost in physical energy that allowed him to enjoy life again.

Over the next few months, James's transformation became undeniable. By honoring himself through self-care, releasing expectations from others, and regularly connecting with his Higher Self, he started setting clear boundaries at work and in personal relationships. He reconnected with his passions and began taking deliberate steps toward his purpose, something he hadn't even realized was possible before. James's story shows that consistent application of these tools doesn't just create temporary relief; it produces profound, lasting changes that align your life with your highest potential.

Both Lisa's and James's experiences illustrate a key point: when you actively engage with the practices in this book, the promises I made in Chapter 1—clarity, peace, empowerment, and alignment—aren't abstract concepts. They are attainable realities, waiting for you to take action.

Lisa's, James's, and my own journey all began with a common starting point: recognizing that change was necessary and committing to taking action. Each of these transformations began with small grounding exercises, daily meditations, energy clearing, or self-reflection. Over time, the consistent practice of these tools produced profound results. The easiest starting point for most people is grounding themselves and incorporating short daily meditations. These create immediate shifts in energy, reduce stress, and help you reconnect with your Higher Self. From there, adding energy clearing, chakra balancing, or self-hypnosis amplifies the effects and begins to unlock deeper layers of transformation.

The key takeaway is that you don't need to do everything at once. Begin with what resonates most with you, something achievable and practical, and commit to it daily. These small, consistent actions compound over time, creating the momentum needed to fully experience the promises of clarity, peace, empowerment, and alignment. Your journey begins here, with one intentional step, leading to lasting transformation that mirrors the results Lisa, James, and I have experienced firsthand.

Now that you've seen how powerful these tools can be, it's time to take your transformation even further. Begin by integrating the practices that resonated most with you, whether grounding, daily meditation, chakra balancing, or energy clearing. From there, layer in additional strategies from earlier chapters, such as self-hypnosis, MerKaBa activations, or shamanic healing sessions. Each of these techniques reinforces the others, creating a holistic approach that accelerates your growth and alignment.

Action Steps to Get Started

1. Choose one grounding or meditation practice and commit to it daily, even for just 5–10 minutes.
2. Incorporate energy clearing or chakra balancing into your weekly routine to release stagnant energy and restore balance.
3. Journal your progress; write down shifts in mood, clarity, or insights to track your transformation.
4. Set clear intentions for what you want to achieve spiritually, emotionally, or energetically, and revisit them regularly.
5. Add one new technique from earlier chapters each week to gradually build a toolbox of practices tailored to your needs.

By following these steps and layering in the strategies from this book, you will create a roadmap for lasting change, manifesting the peace, clarity, and empowerment that you've been seeking.

Just as Lisa, James, and countless others have experienced profound transformation, you too can step into this life of clarity, balance, and purpose. The tools, techniques, and practices shared in this chapter and throughout this book are not just theories; they are proven pathways to reclaiming your energy, connecting with your Higher Self, and living in alignment with your deepest desires. The change is possible, and it begins with your commitment to take action.

Remember, transformation is not reserved for a select few; it is available to anyone willing to practice, explore, and engage with their inner power. By applying these strategies consistently, honoring your journey, and staying open to growth, you can achieve the same sense of peace, empowerment, and fulfillment that you've read about in these stories. Your path starts here, and your possibilities are limitless.

You've walked through stories of courage, resilience, and awakening—proof that transformation is possible for anyone willing to begin. Every technique, reflection, and practice you've explored so far has been preparing you for the next stage of your journey. Chapter 12 invites you to gather everything you've learned and step fully into your potential. This is where insight becomes action, healing becomes embodiment, and you begin to live the truth of who you are—confident, clear, and free.

Chapter 12:

Stepping Fully Into Your Potential

When you first picked up this book, you wondered why life felt so heavy, and why, no matter how hard you tried, you still felt disconnected, overwhelmed, or stuck. You may have asked yourself, "Why can't I find clarity, peace, or purpose?" Perhaps you were searching for answers, looking for a way to stop giving your energy away, or longing to reconnect with your true self. You've felt the weight of expectations, the pull of constant distractions, and the frustration of knowing there must be a better way to live, but not yet finding it. This book began as a guide to help you reclaim your key, step out of the chaos, and start creating a life that aligns with your deepest desires.

By now, you've explored the tools, practices, and insights shared in the previous chapters, and it's time to see how they come together to fulfill the promises made in Chapter 1. These weren't abstract hopes; they were the foundation for everything that followed. Remember, those promises were not empty; they were a roadmap to transformation: to reclaim your energy, release old patterns, reconnect with your Higher Self, and step into a life filled with clarity, purpose, and peace. The key is action. Each meditation, energy-clearing practice, grounding exercise, or self-hypnosis session compounds, building momentum toward the outcomes you've been seeking. By committing to these practices consistently and applying them intentionally, the promises you read about empowerment, balance, healing, and alignment will not only become possible but inevitable.

Earlier in the book, you met Megan, who had been struggling with constant overwhelm and disconnection from herself. She felt drained by her responsibilities, stuck in patterns of people-pleasing, and completely unsure of how to reclaim her energy or purpose. Megan committed to a daily routine of grounding exercises, chakra balancing, and meditation, along with setting clear boundaries and practicing self-care. Within a few weeks, she began noticing a profound shift: her anxiety lessened, her relationships became more balanced, and she started feeling a sense of clarity and empowerment she hadn't experienced in years.

By the end of a few months, Megan was not only more present in her daily life but had also rediscovered her own voice and sense of direction. The promises of the book—reclaiming energy, releasing old patterns, and stepping into alignment with one's Higher Self—were fully coming to life for her. Her transformation illustrates exactly what is possible when the tools and practices shared in this book are applied consistently and intentionally. Megan's story is a living example that the changes you seek are attainable, and your own journey can reflect the same breakthroughs.

Here's a concise synopsis of the big-picture action steps from the previous chapters:

1. Reconnect with Yourself – Prioritize self-care, release expectations from others, and honor your own needs and boundaries.
2. Ground and Align – Spend time in nature, practice grounding exercises, and cultivate a connection with Mother Earth, Father Sky, and your Higher Self.
3. Clear Energy – Cleanse your space, yourself, and your belongings using tools like sage, palo santo, bells, or crystals to remove stagnant or negative energy.
4. Balance and Activate – Work with chakra balancing, Reiki, meditation, and MerKaBa activations to restore harmony within your energy systems.
5. Release Limiting Patterns – Use shamanic healing, hypnosis, or self-hypnosis to identify and release past trauma, old programming, or energetic blocks.
6. Integrate Daily Practices – Consistently apply the techniques and rituals that resonate with you, creating a sustainable routine for ongoing alignment, clarity, and empowerment.

Taken together, these steps form a holistic roadmap to reclaim your energy, awaken your inner power, and live a life aligned with your highest purpose.

Putting these steps into action begins with intentionality and consistency. Start by choosing one or two practices that resonate most with you, perhaps a daily grounding walk, a short meditation, or a simple energy-clearing ritual. Set aside dedicated time each day, even just ten or fifteen minutes, to fully engage in these practices without distractions. As you gain confidence, layer in additional tools like chakra balancing, Reiki, or self-hypnosis. Keep a journal to track your progress, insights, and shifts in energy, emotions, or clarity. The key is to move deliberately, consistently, and with an open mind. Small, daily actions compound over time, creating profound transformation and helping you embody the alignment, peace, and purpose you've been seeking.

You are capable of reclaiming your power, your clarity, and your inner peace. Each step you take, no matter how small, brings you closer to the life you truly desire.

Affirm to yourself daily: I am grounded, I am aligned, I am open to receiving my highest potential. I release what no longer serves me. I trust my inner guidance and honor my journey.

Know that the tools and practices you have learned are always available to you, and with intention and commitment, you can create lasting transformation. Believe in yourself, embrace your growth, and step boldly into the life that is waiting for you.

As you continue your journey of healing, growth, and self-discovery, remember that you don't have to walk this path alone. If you feel called to go deeper, I invite you to explore my offerings at thekeytoyou.com, where you'll find resources, guidance, and services to support your spiritual awakening and personal transformation. You can also visit my other website, mysticglitz.com, to enhance your practice and book services that are tailored to your unique journey. Whether through Reiki, hypnotherapy, shamanic healing, spiritual coaching, or the many other modalities I offer, my intention is always to walk beside you as you uncover your highest potential. These additional services are designed to meet you where you are, providing powerful support as you integrate the practices from this book into your daily life. Together, we can help you step into alignment, clarity, and the life of purpose you were always meant to live.

Thank you for journeying through these pages and for the courage it takes to look within, heal, and grow. Each moment you spend reconnecting with yourself ripples outward—touching others with presence, compassion, and authenticity. Remember, transformation is not a single event but a lifelong unfolding, guided by your willingness to keep showing up for yourself with love and intention.

To continue your journey, visit thekeytoyou.com to explore more tools, programs, and inspiration for living aligned with your Highest Self.

About the Author

Rebecca Hejma is a seasoned spiritual guide, intuitive healer, and the founder of The Key to You: Unlock Your Inner Self, a healing practice rooted in ancient wisdom, modern tools, and soul remembrance. For many years, Rebecca has dedicated her life to helping others reconnect with their inner truth, clear energetic blocks, and reclaim the sacred key to their highest potential.

With a deep passion for learning and growth, Rebecca weaves together a powerful blend of modalities, including shamanic coaching, energy healing, hypnotherapy, and intuitive soul work. She holds numerous certifications across spiritual and holistic disciplines, including Akashic Records Guidance, Reiki Master-Teacher, MerKaBa mastery, and Earth Medicine, just to name a few. Her work is known for its high standards of integrity, compassion, and heartfelt presence.

Rebecca believes that the Universe holds the answers we seek and that by learning to trust its rhythms, we open ourselves to healing, clarity, and miraculous transformation.

She says, *I have learned that believing and trusting in the universe has led me to many miraculous opportunities.*

Having walked the path of disconnection and rediscovery herself, Rebecca understands what it means to give away your power and how to reclaim it. She guides her clients to identify the root cause of their struggles, whether in relationships, career, spiritual alignment, or personal growth, and empowers them with practical tools to come back into balance.

In a world that moves too fast and asks too much, Rebecca offers a return to what truly matters: presence, peace, and purpose. Through her work, she reminds us that we are not lost; we've simply forgotten. And the key to coming home is already within.